C000141477

FOOD FOR DIABETES

RECIPES&PREPARATION

Publisher's Notes:
Diabetes is a serious medical condition that should always be diagnosed and treated by appropriate professionals. This book can only provide helpful information, in support of professional advice and care, to be adapted to suit your individual circumstances. Neither the author nor the publisher can be held responsible for any claim or damage arising out of the use, or misuse, of the information and suggestions made in this book.

Raw or semi-cooked eggs should not be consumed by babies, toddlers, pregnant or breastfeeding women, the elderly or those suffering from a chronic illness.

Wendy Hobson (author) is a well-seasoned writer and editor who specializes in cookery, practical crafts and life skills. She has worked with some of the top names in the business and has many published books to her name, including the *Traditional Home Baking* series, *Classic 1000 Cakes* and *Cooking for One*, as well as editing credit on books such as *Healthy Food for Vegetarian Kids* and *Your Wheat-free Gluten-free Diet Plan*.

Carolyn Humphries (co-author) began her career as a chef, then moved into journalism and has published a shelf full of books, including many offering exciting eating for those on special diets, such as *The Good Gut Diet*, *GI Diet for Life*, *Gluten-free Bread and Cakes* and *Grown in Britain Cookbook*.

Publisher & Creative Director: Nick Wells
Commissioning Editor: Polly Prior
Senior Project Editor: Catherine Taylor
Editorial Assistant: Taylor Bentley
Copy Editor: Adèle Linderholm
Art Director: Mike Spender
Layout Design: Jane Ashley
Digital Design & Production: Chris Herbert

Special thanks to Dawn Laker, Jeremy Werner, Frances Bodiam.

FLAME TREE PUBLISHING
6 Melbray Mews, Fulham,
London SW6 3NS, United Kingdom
www.flametreepublishing.com

This edition published 2019

Copyright © 2019 Flame Tree Publishing Ltd

19 21 23 22 20
1 3 5 7 9 10 8 6 4 2

ISBN: 978-1-78755-313-2

All rights reserved. No part of this publication may be reproduced, stored in a retrieval system, or transmitted in any form or by any means, electronic, mechanical, photocopying, recording or otherwise, without the prior written permission of the publisher.

A copy of the CIP data for this book is available from the British Library.

Printed in China

Images: © StockFood and the following: 80 Gräfe & Unzer Verlag/Kramp + Gölling; 89 Short, Jonathan; 93, 111, 120, 149 Morgans, Gareth; 94, 188 PhotoCuisine/ Lawton, Becky; 114 Wissing, Michael; 119, 128, 138 Great Stock!; 123 Joy Skipper FoodStyling; 130 Arras, Klaus; 135 Eising Studio - Food Photo & Video; 147 Linsell, Samantha; 160 Westermann, Jan-Peter; 163 Meyer-Rebentisch, Dr. Karen; 177, 216 Takacs, Aniko; 179 Guth Linse, Tine; 193 Hendey, Magdalena; 198 McAfee, Tim; 205 Gräfe & Unzer Verlag/Liebenstein, Jana; 215 Strokin, Yelena. Courtesy Shutterstock.com and the following: 2, 57tr Sunny Forest; 6br zarzamora; 6bl Khongtham; 7bl lzf; 7br IriGri; 11t, 59t, 141 Lisovskaya Natalia; 11br vchal; 11bl mythja; 12t, 36b wavebreakmedia; 12br Flotsam; 12bl fizkes; 14bl Pashu Ta Studio; 14br Pixel-Shot; 15br Proxima Studio; 15bl Photographee.eu; 17t, 26bl, 27br, 39t Rawpixel.com; 17b 4pm production; 18b, 36tl Jacob Lund; 18t Nok Lek; 21tr LightField Studios; 21bl Monkey Business Images; 21tl SUPREEYA-ANON; 21br siam.pukkato; 23t nikitabuida; 23b Halfpoint; 25tl YAKOBCHUK VIACHESLAV; 25tr Nastina; 25b goodluz; 26vr George Rudy; 27bl GP Studio; 28, 35, 43t, 168, 187, 224 Kiian Oksana; 30b, 53bl, 57br, front cover Antonina Vlasova; 30t marilyn barbone; 33tr Arina P Habich; 33b nadianb; 33tl, 40br, 43br, 59bl Foxys Forest Manufacture; 36tr Milles Studio; 39b Elena Veselova; 40t Okrasyuk; 40bl Roman Debree; 43bl iko; 45br Yuliia Hurzhos; 45bl Olga Miltsova; 45tl KucherAV; 45tr Megan Betteridge; 47t UfaBizPhoto; 47b baibaz; 48tl zi3000; 48tr Sea Wave; 48bl Indian Food Images; 48br Josie Grant; 51tl Avdeukphoto; 51b, 101, 113, 150, 154, 159 Magdanatka; 51tr Dariia Belkina; 53tr Ekaterina Kondratova; 53br Wiktory; 53tl AS Food studio; 54t Alexander Prokopenko; 54b Rimma Bondarenko; 57bl Jan Wischnewski; 57tl Elena Demyanko; 59br, 197 Anna Shepulova; 60bl Ekaterina Markelova; 60t Liudmyla Yaremenko; 60br Fascinadora; 63t Oleksandra Naumenko; 63bl lalcreative; 63bl Maria Shumova; 64t kitty; 64bl Africa Studio; 64br Lightspring; 67tr, 98 Elena Trukhina; 67b Dani Vincek; 67tl Maria Borodulina; 69t Elena Eryomenko; 69b Timolina; 70 maxtimofeev; 75 Lilia Kandrashevich; 77 & back cover top left, 84 Brent Hofacker; 79 Anna Hoychuck; 83 & back cover top right Olga Nayashkova; 87 Martin Rettenberger; 97 Valeria Aksakova; 103 Jacob Blount; 105 & back cover bottom right Alphonsine Sabine; 106 Damada; 127, 173 Robyn Mackenzie; 137 comeirrez; 143 Barbara Dudzinska; 152 marcin jucha; 167 olepeshkina; 171 Sandhya Hariharan; 174 sarsmis; 180 MariaKovaleva; 191 Andreea Craciun; 195 Aksenya; 201 anna.q; 206 Elena Mayne; 209 & back cover bottom left Yakky; 210 Losangela; 212 alicja neumiler; 219 Gudafuda; 220 Amallia Eka; and small watercolour illustrations throughout: Le Panda and Paket.

FOOD FOR DIABETES
RECIPES & PREPARATION

Wendy Hobson
with Carolyn Humphries

FLAME TREE
PUBLISHING

CONTENTS

INTRODUCTION

Diabetes is a growing problem in the world. In 1980, an already considerable 4.7 per cent of adults in the West suffered from the disease, amounting to 108 million people (World Health Organization). By 2014, this had risen to 8.5 per cent, a staggering 422 million.

Whether you have been recently diagnosed with diabetes, have been living with the condition or, perhaps, have been told that you are pre-diabetic so at risk of developing the disease, now is the time to take action. For those who are obese or overweight, changing to a healthier diet and lifestyle is also the most reliable way to achieve and maintain a healthy weight. If you know you don't do enough physical activity or you should shed a few pounds, this is the way to go. If you review your lifestyle and your diet and make positive changes, you can improve your health both in the short and long term.

This is not a medical textbook. It provides some straightforward information to help you understand your condition and, more importantly, the key things you can do to stay healthy and active. Additionally, it includes a selection of interesting, tasty and easy recipes. Combining these into a healthy, nutritious, balanced diet will help to minimize, or possibly even reverse, the effects of diabetes – just by following a healthy, balanced diet! Breads, bakes and sweet treats are usually made from refined ingredients that we find hard to resist. Eating them piles on the weight, saps energy and suppresses the immune system. So, here I am providing you with mouthwatering alternatives made from superfood ingredients.

These recipes not only give you a nutrient boost, but also provide a super-healthy alternative when those cravings for sweets and carbs hit. Made with healthy sugars, complex carbohydrates and complete proteins, these dishes are more satisfying than the refined and processed kind, without the energy dip or bloated after-effects. Have fun with superfoods. Mix them up, sprinkle them on and stir them in! Healthy cooking should be about maximum nutrition, ultimate tastiness and minimum fuss for all the family, so enjoy exploring these recipes and discovering more about superfoods.

WHAT YOU NEED TO KNOW

WHAT IS DIABETES?

If we understand how our body should work, it makes it easier to understand what we need to do to keep it functioning well. This is a very simple explanation of what goes wrong with our system if we have diabetes.

HOW THE SYSTEM SHOULD WORK

We all need energy to function – not just for conscious physical activity but for unconscious actions such as breathing, growing and digesting – and we get our energy from our food. The carbohydrates in the food we eat are broken down and converted into a type of sugar called glucose, which then enters the bloodstream. However, glucose cannot pass directly into the cells where it is needed; it needs the help of a hormone called insulin, which is produced in the pancreas. When the body detects that there is a high level of glucose in the blood – after we have eaten, for example – it triggers the release of insulin from the pancreas. The insulin attaches to the cells and enables them to absorb the glucose and use it to supply the body with essential energy. If the body has more glucose than it needs, insulin helps store it in the liver and releases it when it is required, keeping the amount of glucose level in the blood, as it should be.

WHEN IT GOES WRONG

Diabetes is a chronic condition in which the pancreas fails to produce enough insulin, or the body is unable to use the insulin it does produce. This results in a build-up of glucose in the bloodstream. There are two main types of diabetes that affect the majority of people suffering from the condition: Type 1 and Type 2. (There are other, rarer types, such as gestational diabetes.)

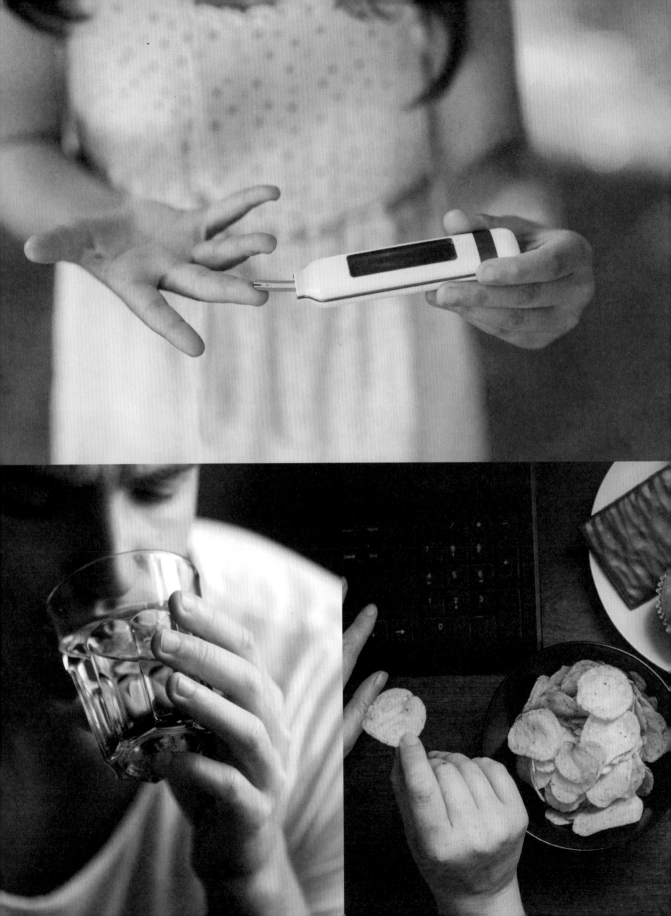

Type 1:

This is a life-long condition, often diagnosed in childhood or youth, in which the body attacks the cells in the pancreas so that it can no longer produce insulin. Its cause is unknown, but it affects 10 per cent of people with diabetes in the UK.

Type 2:

In this type of diabetes, lifestyle factors – such as an unbalanced, high-calorie diet and lack of exercise – have made the pancreas work so hard it is unable to release enough insulin to process the glucose effectively. This can affect people of any age and is increasingly being diagnosed in young people.

SYMPTOMS

There are a number of symptoms of diabetes, although around half of people have no significant symptoms when they are diagnosed with Type 2 diabetes.

- Since the body cannot pass the excess glucose to the cells, it tries to get rid of it through the kidneys, causing the need to pee frequently.

- This can make you feel really thirsty.

- Because the body is not getting enough energy, you are likely to feel tired.

- You may get genital itching or thrush, because all that sugary pee is the perfect breeding ground for a fungal infection.

- Your body may try to get energy from its fat stores, so you may lose weight.

- Other possible symptoms include eyesight problems or wounds taking longer to heal.

POTENTIAL COMPLICATIONS

Diabetes is a very serious condition, with many potential complications – hence the importance of making changes to your lifestyle. High glucose levels in the blood can cause problems for your heart, eyes, feet and kidneys. Untreated, in the worst-case scenarios, this can lead to blindness, heart disease or gangrene, which can lead to limb amputation.

Hypoglycaemia

Even if you are generally keeping your blood sugar levels steady, occasionally they may fall, and this causes hypoglycaemia. You may tremble, sweat and go pale, have a high pulse rate and palpitations, tingly lips, blurred vision or a headache, feel hungry, tired, tearful, anxious or be unable to concentrate.

You need to take something sweet – something like three dextrose tablets, five jelly beans or a small carton of fruit juice – then seek medical advice. In extreme cases, you may be so disorientated you are unaware you are having an attack; always have an emergency sugar fix with you so someone else can give it to you if necessary.

The opposite of this is hyperglycaemia, which occurs when your blood sugar levels are too high. You may feel tired, have a headache or stomach ache, feel thirsty or need to pee. Drink plenty of water or sugar-free drinks and seek medical advice.

MANAGING DIABETES

For Type 1 diabetes, regular supplies of insulin to the body – either by injection or through a pump – are essential. People with Type 1 diabetes will need to test their blood sugar levels frequently and are likely to be under fairly close medical supervision.

In addition to professional care, a well-balanced diet and active lifestyle will make a huge difference to maintaining general good health.

For Type 2 diabetes, patients will also be medically supervised, but they may find that a change to a healthier, balanced diet and a more active lifestyle can be enough on its own to manage the condition, or even reverse the effects. If this is not successful, then tablets or injections may become necessary.

MYTH-BUSTERS

Type 2 is a less serious version of Type 1: **FALSE**

Diabetes is a serious condition. Type 2 may be easier to manage, but it cannot be ignored or the consequences can be equally damaging.

People with diabetes are more likely to be unwell: **FALSE**

If you manage your diabetes sensibly, there's no reason you should be more prone to minor illnesses.

People with diabetes mustn't drive: **FALSE**

Anyone with a chronic condition should report it to the DVLA or equivalent local organization. Providing the condition is well managed and your eyesight reaches the required standard, there is no need to give up driving.

A HEALTHY LIFESTYLE

Many people with diabetes find they don't need medication if they follow an active routine and eat a varied, balanced diet. And there is no need for your regime to differ from the rest of the family because the principles of a healthy lifestyle are the same for everyone.

THE CHANGE STARTS NOW

However healthy your current lifestyle, it is likely that you will be able to make improvements. In the first place, be honest with yourself about where you are starting from.

- How many meals a day do you have? Do you often have 'seconds'?

- What are your favourite foods?

- Do you eat between meals? What do you snack on?

- Do you smoke? How much?

- Do you drink? How much and how frequently?

- How often do you exercise? What kind of exercise do you enjoy? Is there anything you have always wanted to try?

- What are your most unhealthy habits? What are your most healthy habits?

- What do you dread most about making changes? How good are you at rising to a challenge?

There is no advantage in being anything other than completely honest because this is all about finding what is right for you – it's not a competition. With your particular needs in mind, you can see more quickly which changes will benefit you the most.

GET MOVING

Especially for those of us with sedentary jobs, cars, TVs and a comfy sofa, there is plenty of scope to improve our activity levels. The crucial thing is that we will be successful only if we enjoy what we are doing. If joining a gym or going for a run is your idea of hell on Earth, don't waste your time and money.

Start small and start straightaway. Factor in some exercise to be a natural part of your day so you don't even think about it: walk up and downstairs a few times a day; take the stairs instead of the easier options; walk to the shops to pick up some milk. Leave the car at home if where you are going is less than a 15-minute walk away. If you do drive, park at the farthest end of the car park from your destination.

While all that becomes part of your routine, find out about local exercise options (Google it or visit your local library) and then try out something you like the look of. Not enjoying it after a few attempts? Try something else.

- **For the team players:** You are spoiled for choice as there so many local clubs and leisure centres with teams at all levels, from a run-around and a laugh to high-quality players. Rugby, football, netball, soccer, hockey, basketball ...

- **My playing days are over:** Are you sure? What about walking football, bowling or archery? Or why not volunteer to coach some youngsters?

- **I prefer one-person sports**: As with team sports, the choice is yours. Go for badminton, tennis, squash ...

- **I want to be alone:** You could love being alone with your thoughts on a daily run, a swim, or competing against yourself in a gym workout where you can get expert guidance to spur you on.

- **I like exercises to music:** Dancing is great exercise. What about aerobics, body pump, body groove, line dancing, Ceroc, salsa, Zumba, ballroom dancing or aquarobics?

- **I just like being at home:** Get an exercise bike and set it up in front of the TV or put on your headphones and listen to music or podcasts. There's no need to spend a fortune on equipment – look at your local or online secondhand outlets. Get out in the garden and do some digging and weeding. You don't have to be wearing sports kit to get exercise.

- **I enjoy communing with nature:** Join a walking group, such as the Ramblers, or volunteer for a local conservation group that maintains a local park.

- **I want something more mindful:** Try a Pilates or yoga class. You'll still get a good workout.

GIVE UP SMOKING

From a health point of view, smoking makes no sense for anyone. For those with a chronic condition, such as diabetes, it is even more damaging. There are no 'ifs' or 'buts', the only issue is 'how'. First, if you are a smoker, define your reason for giving up: so you can live a longer, healthier life and avoid a horrible death.

Tell everyone you have given up and ask them to help you. Circulate it on social media. Get everyone onside.

Think about the triggers that make you crave a cigarette and try to take yourself away from those tempations.

- **Want something to do with your hands when watching TV?** Learn to knit or crochet, get an adult colouring or puzzle book.

- **Reach for a cigarette when you have a beer? Drink in places where you can't smoke.** Stop buying alcohol to drink at home for a while.

- **Smoke when you are nervous?** Learn some breathing exercises or meditation techniques.

- **Light up when someone else does?** Keep away from smokers. Ask friends not to offer you cigarettes.

- **Really can't give up?** Try e-cigarettes to wean you off gradually.

You don't have to tackle it alone. Contact your pharmacist or your local healthcare provider for help and advice. Take advantage of patches, gum, stop-smoking books or programmes, podcasts or hypnosis.

If you can't do it for yourself, do it for someone else: your parents, a child or a grandchild, a partner – even to honour the memory of someone who was precious to you.

One thing you must not do is grab unhealthy snacks instead of a cigarette or you will pile on the pounds. If you must nibble, choose a handful of berries, raw nuts or vegetable sticks or plain, unsalted and unsweetened popcorn.

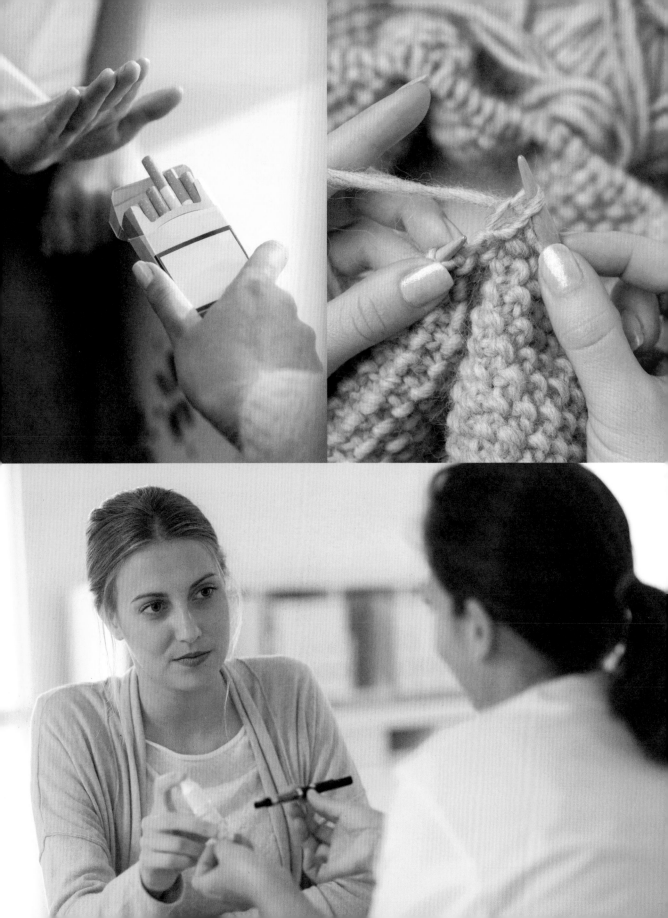

MAINTAIN A HEALTHY WEIGHT

Your body mass index (BMI) tells you whether you are the correct weight for your height, sex and age. There are plenty of BMI calculators and handy charts online – you just need to know your height and weight.

The best way to lose weight safely is to increase your level of exercise and follow a healthy, balanced diet, as outlined in the following pages. Check what your calorie intake should be (typically is a maximum of 2,000 for women or 2,500 for men) and eat three sensible meals a day.

Cut Down on Alcohol

Alcohol contains a lot of sugar – the calories in alcohol are called 'empty calories' because there is no nutritional goodness in them. It can therefore create a massive

spike in your blood sugar levels for no benefit, which is not what we are looking for. Enjoy it, but keep your intake moderate. The recommended safe level is 14 units per week.

MYTH-BUSTERS

People with diabetes can't take part in sports: **FALSE**

Quite the reverse is true – just do it!

People with diabetes can't travel: **FALSE**

Only in some circumstances. If you have specific circulatory problems, or other medical problems, you should consult your doctor. Otherwise you can travel as much as anyone else.

EAT WELL WITH DIABETES

A diet for diabetes is simply a healthy, balanced diet. There's no need for you to eat differently from the rest of the family; if you apply these principles, then it will benefit everyone. So think of any changes as positive changes. Nothing is banned. Just concentrate on all the great foods you can enjoy and how much better you will feel.

WHAT IS THE IDEAL DIET?

The aim of your diet is to eat the right foods in the right proportions and quantities to supply all your nutritional needs. This will help to maintain the glucose in your blood at an even level to provide the energy for your busy life. This is important for everyone, but especially for those with diabetes, as their mechanisms for keeping blood sugar levels correct are not working as they should.

There are a few easy-to-understand principles. There's more detail in the rest of this introduction.

- **Eat the right balance of food types:** Starchy carbohydrates, proteins, fats, fruit and vegetables, fibre.

- **Eat plenty of vegetables and fruit:** Buy seasonally and locally for the best quality, but remember that frozen or canned vegetables, without added sugar or salt, are just as nutritious as fresh.

- **Choose starchy (complex) carbohydrates:** These foods, particularly wholegrains, take longer for your body to process than simple carbohydrates and this helps to stabilize your blood sugar levels.

- **Avoid refined (simple) carbohydrates (added sugars):** All types of white or brown sugar, honey and syrup will cause that unwanted surge in your blood sugar levels. Naturally occurring sugars, such as in fruit, vegetables and milk, are okay (because of the benefits of their other nutrients).

- **Include a good proportion of protein:** Meat, fish, poultry, eggs, pulses, nuts and seeds are needed for growth and repair.

- **Eat dairy foods in moderation:** Milk, yogurt and cheese will aid strong teeth and bones, but limit the full-fat varieties.

- **Your body needs some fat:** Make sure it is not too much and is mainly unsaturated or monounsaturated.

- **Cut down on salt:** Replace it with herbs and naturally flavoursome ingredients.

- **Include plenty of dietary fibre:** Both soluble and insoluble fibre contribute to keeping your blood sugar levels even and your gut working effectively.

- **Cut down on processed and white refined foods:** They contain high levels of salt, sugar and preservatives, and are very quickly absorbed.

- **Drink:** Drink plenty of water. Limit fruit juice to one small glass a day as part of a meal.

- **Serve reasonable portion sizes:** Then you will reach and maintain a healthy weight.

EAT THE RIGHT BALANCE OF FOOD TYPES

Nothing is banned on a diet for diabetes, but some foods should be regulars in your diet and others occasional treats. If you aim for the right food balance in every meal, then overall, you are going to get it right. You will soon learn how strictly you have to adhere to the plan, depending on your specific condition, and whether the occasional badly balanced meal will really affect you.

Your meals should be made up of approximately:

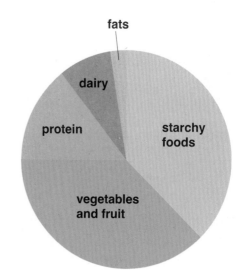

- 33 per cent starchy foods
- 33 per cent vegetables and fruit
- 18 per cent protein
- 12 per cent dairy
- 4 per cent fats

Ready meals and other convenience foods can contain high levels of salt, sugar, preservatives, flavourings and additives that your body doesn't need. Include as much fresh food as you can in your diet, using cans and packs thoughtfully. A can of sweetcorn in water, for example, contains just sweetcorn and water; a can of tomatoes contains ... tomatoes, so they are both good additions to your diet. But a package of instant vegetable soup will have a long list of ingredients that are hardly worth even straining to read.

We'll look at the details of the individual foods on the following pages.

DRINK PLENTY OF WATER

Keep your body well hydrated and it will work much more efficiently.
Recommendations vary on how much water you should drink every day but
1.2 litres/2 pints/5 cups (or 6–8 glasses) is considered about right.

You could limit caffeinated tea or coffee and replace it with naturally caffeine-free
teas, such as rooibos, as well as herbal teas or decaffeinated varieties.

GET INTO GOOD EATING HABITS

Many of us tend to rush our meals, eat on the go and snack more than is good for us.
Here are some top tips for eating well:

- **Plan your meals:** This will help you get a good balance and avoid temptation.

- **Make a shopping list and don't shop when you are hungry:** You'll be less tempted to
buy junk food.

- **Keep a store cupboard:** If you always have the essentials for a healthy meal (such
as canned vegetables, fish and pulses, frozen peas and chicken, herbs and
spices, pasta), you won't be so tempted by unhealthy quick fixes or takeaways.

- **Present food well:** Attractive colours, textures and garnishes make the experience
more enjoyable.

- **Double up:** Make extra and freeze portions for another day.

- **Eat at regular intervals:** This is particularly important for people with diabetes to
keep blood sugar levels even.

- **Sit down to your meals:** Set the table and make meals a social event.

- **Serve what you need:** Don't use too big a plate and don't pile up food.

- **Eat slowly:** Think about what you are eating and savour the flavours. Put down your knife and fork between mouthfuls.

- **Let it rest:** It takes about 20 minutes for your body to realize it is full, so give it time – don't just rush to find something else to eat.

- **Avoid too much snacking:** It's too easy to eat more than you need, or fill up on snacks and then not enjoy nutritious meals. However, going too long between meals is not good either, particularly for someone with diabetes. If you need a snack to keep you going, choose a rice cake, oat cake, vegetable sticks or a handful of raw, unsalted nuts.

RECOMMENDED PORTION SIZES

Even if you are eating the right proportions of food groups, if you are eating twice as much as you should, you are going to put on weight. You can easily implement portion control without dull and obsessive weighing and measuring. A standard-size dinner plate should be neatly covered, not piled high. Use a standard measuring cup, or a regular teacup, to gauge the correct portion sizes. As a rough guide, one portion of food represents:

- 2 cups of leafy green vegetables
- 1 medium potato
- 1 cup of chopped raw vegetables, fresh fruit, milk or yogurt
- 1½ cups of cooked rice or other grains
- a fist-sized (but not Muhammad Ali's) piece of cooked meat

See the following pages for more details.

Should you be Counting Calories?

Once you get used to the types of foods you should eat and the quantities that are appropriate, you are unlikely to need to bother counting calories. As a starting point, men need about 2,500 calories a day and women need about 2,000 calories a day.

MYTH-BUSTERS

People with diabetes shouldn't eat fruit. **FALSE**

Fruit does contain sugar, but most fruits don't increase your blood sugar as quickly as a slice of bread.

You can only eat 'diabetic' foods: **FALSE**

Because they are often high in fat to compensate for low sugar, and use sugar substitutes that are frequently laxative, doctors generally advise against them.

You can't eat sugar: **FALSE**

A healthy balanced diet is low in sugar and contains little or no refined sugar – that doesn't mean going without treats.

Frozen yogurt is better for you than ice cream: **FALSE**

Although sometimes lower in fat, it often has more sugar than a similar ice cream.

People with diabetes can't have carbs: **FALSE**

The right proportion and type of carbohydrate forms an essential part of your diet.

A WELL-BALANCED DIET

Now we are familiar with the basic principles, let's fill in some detail. Here you will learn more about making healthy choices in the range of foods you can enjoy.

FRUIT & VEGETABLES

Fruit and vegetables provide us with vitamins, minerals, antioxidants and fibre.

For colour and nutritional value, you can't beat filling your plate with a selection of fresh vegetables. There are so many different varieties available that you need never run out of ideas (and don't abandon the humble frozen pea or other frozen vegetables; picked and packed to retain all their nutrients, they make a great standby in the freezer).

Since we are constantly being told to eat our five a day, none of us can honestly say we didn't know that. It is perhaps less well known that we should actually eat *at least* five portions every day, preferably ten. Eat a rainbow of vegetables and fruit not just because they look great but because the different colours have a variety of health benefits. Try to buy seasonally for the best quality, flavour and nutritional value, and buy locally to cut down on the food miles and the time our ingredients have to spend in refrigeration.

Fruits do contain sugar but it is natural sugar, which is different from the 'empty calories' you get from added sugar in cakes, cookies and alcohol. Fruits provide essential vitamins, minerals and the all-important soluble fibre (and insoluble fibre if you eat the skins).

Recommended Portion Sizes

A portion of fruit or vegetables is roughly what you can fit into the palm of your hand.
You should have at least five a day, spread out through the day.

apple, pear or banana	1 medium
avocado	½
broccoli or cauliflower florets	8
cucumber	5-cm/2-inch piece
dried peas, beans and lentils, cooked	3 heaped tbsp
fruit juice (limit to one portion a day)	150 ml/5 fl oz/⅔ cup
grapes	1 handful
kiwifruit	2
mango or pawpaw	½
melon	1 large slice
mushrooms	1 portobello (large cremini), 4 large cup or 14 baby button
onion	1 medium
peas or sweetcorn	3 heaped tbsp
pineapple, fresh	1 large slice
pineapple rings in natural juice (canned)	2 rings, or 12 chunks
plums	2 medium
raisins, sultanas (golden raisins), currants or dried cranberries	1 heaped tbsp
root vegetables or squashes, diced or sliced and cooked	3 heaped tbsp
salad, mixed	1 individual-size salad bowlful
satsumas, clementines or tangerines	2 small
strawberries	7 medium
tomato	1 medium or 7 cherry

CARBOHYDRATES

Carbohydrates are the foods that give us energy most quickly and efficiently. If you have diabetes, it is particularly important to be careful with your carb intake, but this is not quite as straightforward as it might be because of the complex nature of the carbohydrate food group.

Types of Carbohydrate

There are two types of carbohydrate: complex 'starchy' carbs that are converted into glucose at differing rates by the body, some slowly, some more rapidly; and simple 'sugar' carbs that are absorbed very quickly.

Those that are absorbed slowly are said to have a low glycaemic index (GI). These are an important part of a healthy diet and are particularly helpful for people with diabetes. Those that are absorbed quickly have a high GI, meaning that they are not helpful because they will cause spikes in the blood sugar levels.

The Glycaemic Index

The Glycaemic Index measures how quickly the carbs are converted into glucose in the bloodstream as measured against pure glucose. Glucose is 100 (as it is absorbed instantly) and foods such as meat or fish that contain no carbohydrates are rated at 0. Most foods that contain some carbs are rated somewhere in between.

Simple 'sugar' carbs, on the whole, have a high GI: these include cakes, cookies, sweetened breakfast cereals, ready meals, processed foods and foods made with finely ground flours.

'Starchy' carbs tend to have a lower GI (55 or less): these include unprocessed wholegrains, pulses and many fruit and vegetables (except very sweet ones, such as ripe melon and dates).

As well as wheat-based wholegrain bread (like granary), there are also plenty of different types of wholegrain carbs you can try, such as oats (great at lowering cholesterol too), barley, freekeh, quinoa, corn, buckwheat, millet, brown rice and couscous.

Other Factors

This simple definition of GI, however, is not the whole picture, as GI is complicated by a number of other factors:

- **Ripeness:** Overripe fruit has a higher GI than less ripe fruit because much of the carb has already been converted into sugar in the ripening process. That's why ripe fruit tastes sweeter.

- **How finely ground the grains are:** The finer the flour, the quicker it is turned into glucose and absorbed – so the higher the GI. For this reason, while you might think wholemeal (whole grain) flour, and therefore wholemeal bread, is low GI, in fact because the whole grain is finely ground so that the body can process it quickly, it is high GI. But bread full of whole seeds and grains has a lower GI because it takes longer for the body to break down the grains into sugar.

- **Has the food already been processed?** Processed food – whether processed in a factory or in your kitchen – will have a higher GI than raw or less processed. Instant mashed potato has a higher GI than fresh mash because the potato has already been broken down into a powder. But freshly made mash, as it is crushed, will have a higher GI than steamed or boiled potatoes since part of the breakdown of the food has begun.

- **Is the food high in fat?** Some appropriately chosen fats are essential in the diet, and, in fact, since fat prevents rapid absorption of glucose, it helps to keep your blood sugar levels even. Therefore, some foods that you might expect to be high GI are actually low GI because the fat they contain slows the absorption of the carbs. This is true of crisps (potato chips) and chocolate. However, they are still high in unwanted fat so, despite being low GI, should be for occasional treats only.

- **What is the carbohydrate being cooked or eaten with?** Mixing fat or protein with the carb when cooking also slows down its absorption rate, whether the fat is in the food itself or served with it: a baked potato with some grated cheese will not be absorbed as quickly as the potato on its own. It is better to spread a slice of white bread with a little butter that will not raise your blood sugar levels as much as eating the bread on its own.

- **How easily does the carb break down when cooked?** Most rice and pasta will have a lower GI if it is cooked to *al dente*, so still has 'bite'. However, basmati breaks down more slowly than, for instance, sticky white jasmine rice, and therefore has a lower GI. In general, wholegrain, brown varieties have a lower GI than white. Raw carrots have a much lower GI than when cooked. Baked potatoes – cooked long and slow so a lot of the starch is already converted into sugar before we eat them – have a high GI. Baked sweet potatoes, yams or plantains have a lower GI than ordinary potatoes, and boiled even lower than baked.

- **What is the fibre content?** Some starchy foods, particularly whole, unprocessed grains, have a low GI because their high fibre content inhibits absorption.

- **How much you eat:** One jelly bean won't do much to your blood sugar levels but if you eat a whole packet...

Recommended Portion Sizes

You should have at least five of these portions of carbohydrate-rich foods a day, spread through the day and focusing on low GI.

bread, preferably wholegrain	1 slice
breakfast cereal	3 tbsp
couscous, barley, quinoa, millet	2 heaped tbsp
pasta or noodles, boiled *al dente*	3 heaped tbsp
porridge oats (oatmeal), cooked (50 g/1¾ oz/½ cup raw)	1 medium bowl
potato	½ medium
rice, cooked (preferably basmati or brown)	2 heaped tbsp
sweet potato	½ large

PROTEIN

Foods that are high in protein are essential to build and replace muscle. Important sources of protein are lean meat, fish, eggs, pulses, beans and nuts.

You can include all kinds of lean poultry and meat in your diet, trimming off the visible fat before you cook, but go easy on red meat (lamb, beef and pork) and processed meats (like ham, sausages and salami).

White and oily fish are excellent sources of easily digestible protein. Variety is the key. Include canned fish, such as sardines, tuna or salmon, preferably in water rather than brine or oil.

Pulses also provide protein, so serve them on their own or use them to bulk out other dishes, such as soups and casseroles. Try chickpeas (garbanzo beans), red kidney beans, cannellini beans, butter (lima) beans and lentils. It is cheaper to buy them uncooked, then

soak and cook them according to the instructions on the packet. However, it is always worth having a few cans in the store cupboard as they are quick and easy to use hot or cold.

Eggs are great served any way you like them, although if you scramble or fry, use a nonstick pan and minimal oil or butter.

Replace your usual snacks with nutritious raw nuts and seeds, or add them to salads or garnishes. Toasting them in a dry frying pan before you use them gives them a richer flavour and more crunch. Unsalted, unsweetened nut butters (with no additions – just pulverised nuts) are good spread on oatcakes, rice wafers, on chicory (endive) leaves or stuffed in celery stalks. (You can make your own if you have a high-speed blender.)

Recommended Portion Sizes

You should aim for two or three portions of protein food a day.

cooked beans and pulses, such as red kidney beans, butter (lima) beans, chickpeas (garbanzo beans) or lentils	3–4 tbsp
fish	85–100 g/3–3½ oz
cooked lean meat, such as chicken, beef or pork	60–90 g/ 2–3 oz, or the size of a deck of playing cards
nut or peanut butter (100 per cent nuts)	2 tbsp, or the size of a golf ball
Quorn or tofu or silken tofu	120 g/4 oz, or the size of a billiard ball

DAIRY

Dairy foods are important in your diet for nutrients such as calcium, essential for strong teeth and bones. They also supply protein and some carbohydrates. In general, you should reduce your intake of saturated and animal fats, so make sure you stick to the recommendation below of how much dairy to include.

Many people love to nibble on a piece of cheese, but you may have to restrict your urges here and keep the piece small. For cooking, buy cheeses with a strong flavour, such as Parmesan or a mature Cheddar or Gouda, then you can use less and still get the flavour. Choose naturally lower-fat options, when you can, such as quark, ricotta, mozzarella and feta. For hard cheeses, such as Cheddar, try reduced-fat varieties. Go for reduced-fat or low-fat cream cheese. Also remember that many cheeses are high in salt.

Choose fat-free or low-fat natural yogurt without added sugar – check the labels. This still contains naturally occurring sugar from the milk (lactose), but there is usually less than 5 g/⅛ oz sugar per 100 g/3½ oz yogurt; more than that and it will have been added.

Flavoured yogurts tend to contain added sugar. If you do buy them, make sure you check how much they contain. If they claim to be thick and creamy but low in fat, you can be pretty sure they also contain thickeners (starches) to enhance the texture. If you want to add flavouring, add your own puréed fruit, natural vanilla or chopped toasted, unsalted hazelnuts.

Recommended Portion Sizes

Aim for two or three portions of healthy dairy products a day.

hard cheese, bloom-rinded cheese, such as Camembert	30 g/1 oz/1 small matchbox
low-sugar, low-fat fromage frais or yogurt	125 g/ 4½ oz/1 small pot
reduced-fat or low-fat cream cheese	60 g/2–3 oz/2 small matchboxes
semi-skimmed or skimmed milk	200 ml/7 fl oz/1 glass

Vegan or Dairy Free

You can also replace your dairy products with nut milks and other non-dairy alternatives. Soya products, unsweetened almond milk and oat milk are all readily available in supermarkets, but do make sure you buy the unsweetened varieties. Non-dairy 'milks' contain at least as much calcium as cows' milk, although some are fortified.

FAT

Fats often get a bad press. In moderation and making good choices, fats are not only desirable but essential in your diet for providing energy, constructing cell membranes and as a catalyst for absorbing vitamins and minerals. They also add great flavour to your food.

There are four types of fat: saturated, monounsaturated, polyunsaturated and trans fats.

- **Saturated fat:** Reduce this by trimming off visible fat from meat, not eating the skin of poultry and cutting down on bacon and processed foods. Coconut oil has other health benefits but should still be used sparingly.

- **Monounsaturated fats:** Found in macadamia nuts, olive oil and avocado, all of these have health benefits if eaten in moderation.

- **Polyunsaturated fats:** Including the healthy omega-3 fatty acids that improve hormone health and support brain and muscle function. Use sunflower, rapeseed (canola) or olive oil for cooking and dressings.

- **Trans fats:** These are mostly found in partially hydrogenated oils, so products containing these should be avoided (check labels). They have been solidified by heating, making them the least healthy of all the fats as they can increase LDL cholesterol in the blood. Thankfully, many countries have restricted the use of trans fats.

Have a scraping of butter (a saturated fat) or low-fat spread on bread or toast and add a small drizzle of oil or use an oil spray when cooking or in dressings. Use a nonstick pan and avoid deep-frying.

Recommended Portion Sizes

You should eat no more than 20 g/¾ oz saturated fat a day for women or 30 g/1 oz for men. Some recommended portion sizes are:

butter or margarine	5 g/1 tsp
low-fat spread	10 g/2 tsp
unsaturated oils	5 ml/1 tsp

Food Labelling

The traffic light system of labelling on food packaging in the UK and many other countries indicates whether the food is high, medium or low in calories, fat, saturated fat, sugar and salt by means of red, amber and green panels. This is useful but far from foolproof, so must be used with caution. For example, sending a child off to school with a can of diet cola and a bag of popcorn might give you an array of green lights but nutritionally they are supplying nothing much but air and artificial sweeteners. On the other hand, a creamy yogurt with some chopped raw nuts and prunes would throw up at least three red lights and several ambers, although it is the far healthier choice.

Also be aware of claims such as 'lower fat'. The food must have 30 per cent less fat than a similar product, but it might still contain quite a lot of fat if the original product is high in fat in the first place.

SUGAR

As we know, sugar is a type of carbohydrate, and carbs play an important role in our healthy diet. What we are talking about here is refined sugar, stripped of all its nutrients and offering only empty calories. All this does is to create a spike in your blood sugar levels that is exactly the opposite of what you are trying to achieve.

Fortunately, most high-sugar products are easy to spot: sweets, cakes, chocolate, desserts. You don't have to give them up completely, but they should be an occasional treat. Once you get used to eating less sugar, it will gradually become your norm and you will find that you miss it less and less.

Where Is It Hiding?

Sugar finds its way into all sorts of products, sweet and savoury. Who knew baked beans were high in sugar until they brought out a sugar-free variety? This is one of the reasons to cut down on ready-made foods, but if you do buy them, take a look at the label first.

Pure fruit juice is another source of high quantities of sugar because it is so concentrated and the goodness of the fibre has been taken out. Enjoy just one small glass a day with a meal.

Breakfast cereals, breads, fruit juice drinks (sitting next to the pure juices) and just about every ready meal or TV dinner may have lots of sugar, so always check the labels.

What Can I Have Instead?

Experiment with spices and flavourings to give new flavours to your cooking, such as cinnamon and vanilla that will add natural sweetness.

It is better simply to cut down on sugar rather than replace it with a sugar substitute, but for special occasions and treats, or if you really can't give up sugar in tea or coffee, you could use stevia or another artificial sweetener.

Naturally sweet dried fruit, apple purée or a banana can be used in cooking instead of sugar in both sweet and savoury dishes.

Agave syrup, honey, pomegranate molasses and maple syrup are also natural products for use sparingly. Better to use than refined sugar but still sugar, causing your blood sugar to spike if you use too much.

SALT

Additional salt is not necessary in our food. It enhances the flavours, but it can build up in the body, causing an increase in blood pressure. This has the potential to put a strain on the heart, arteries, kidneys and brain, thereby opening us up to serious health problems such as heart attacks, strokes, dementia and kidney disease. If you stop adding salt when cooking vegetables, for instance, you will soon find you enjoy the actual taste of the vegetable itself and won't miss the salt. Experiment with other flavourings, such as herbs and spices, lemon juice, garlic, celery seeds and dried mushrooms. Make your own stock (bouillon) (*see* page 183) or buy reduced-salt stock cubes, granules, concentrate or ready-made (check the labels) and avoid processed foods. Choose reduced-salt and reduced-sugar condiments, such as ketchup and naturally fermented soy sauce.

Recommended Intake

Adults should eat no more than 6 g/1 tsp salt per day.

FIBRE

There are two types of fibre, both vital to health and well-being.

Soluble fibre is found mainly in fruit, vegetables, pulses and wholegrains – particularly oats, barley and rye, nuts and seeds (especially golden linseed). This type slows the absorption of glucose in the bloodstream and helps keep blood sugar levels constant. It also helps to keep our stools soft and to lower blood-cholesterol levels, thus helping to prevent heart disease.

The second type is insoluble fibre, which used to be known as 'roughage'. This is the type that keeps our gut working efficiently, preventing constipation and other issues. It's found in the membranes of fruit and vegetables, and in the husks of grains, seeds, nuts and pulses.

Recommended Intake

If you are eating the recommended proportions of fresh fruit and vegetables, you should be getting enough fibre.

At-a-glance Choices

Your at-a-glance guide to some of the best food choices.

Swap out	New choice
Minced (ground) beef	Turkey, chicken or soya mince
White bread	Granary or other wholegrain (whole wheat) and seed breads, pumpernickel
Breakfast cereal	Unsweetened muesli, porridge (oatmeal)
Butter	Extra virgin rapeseed (canola) or olive oil
Cheese	Lower-fat cheeses like feta, Parmesan, goat's cheese, mozzarella, Camembert, Edam and cottage cheese
Milk or white chocolate	Dark chocolate with at least 70 per cent cocoa solids (but it is still high in fat, so just one or two squares a day)
Jam	Whole fruit spread sweetened with natural fruit concentrate
Pasta	Pasta with added fibre or wholegrain pasta, and cook al dente
Potatoes	Sweet potatoes, yams or celeriac
White long-grain rice	Basmati or brown rice, cooked al dente, or bulgur wheat, pearl barley or quinoa
Salt	Add plenty of freshly ground black pepper and make use of sweet spices (cumin, cinnamon, nutmeg and paprika
Stock	Choose low-salt varieties, or make your own
Sugar (added)	Use naturally sweet fruit purée (such as stewed dessert apple), mashed banana or dried fruits to add sweetness (for drinks, try stevia sweetener)

PREPARATION & TECHNIQUES

The principles of preparing and cooking a healthy balanced diet are simple – you are looking to retain as much of the goodness in the foods as possible, while preparing attractive, tasty and wholesome meals.

FOOD PREPARATION

Scrub fruits and vegetables and serve them raw when you can. Don't peel them unless the outer layer is inedible. Much of the nutrient value is in or under the skin, which also provides valuable natural fibre. Don't overcook.

Trim meat and poultry of visible fat and skin when possible.

COOKING METHODS

We should all avoid too much fat, so don't deep-fry or roast in added fat very often. For preference, go for boiling, poaching, grilling (broiling), stir-frying or baking.

For meat or poultry, braise, casserole or stew. For occasional grilling (broiling) or roasting, use a rack or a ridged griddle pan so the fat can drain off. Use only a spray of oil to moisten the pan and heat the pan before you add the ingredients. Add a little water if food starts to stick.

Fish is delicious lightly grilled (broiled), poached or baked.

Beans and pulses can be boiled or steamed. Follow the instructions on the packet as some need pre-soaking, and different beans have different cooking times.

PLANNING YOUR MEALS

It is a good idea to plan your meals in advance to make it easier to maintain a balance. Aim for three meals a day – breakfast, light lunch and dinner – and allow yourself one or two healthy snacks. All the recipes for main courses are designed as complete meals in themselves, with accompaniments where relevant. Allow yourself a dessert with dinner, if you like. Or you may want to have your main meal during the day and a lighter meal in the evening.

Eating Out

Obviously, people with diabetes are going to have to be more careful than most when eating out. Choose your restaurant with care in the first place. With most menus now online, you can do a bit of homework before you go, phone ahead or ask the waiter's advice – in most restaurants they will be happy to ask the chef. Make your selections, as far as you can, to match the good principles you have established, and remember to test your blood sugar levels slightly more often than usual to enable adjustments should you have an adverse reaction.

BREAKFASTS

AVOCADO & ALMOND SMOOTHIE
with Spinach

A freshly made smoothie makes a great start to the day, giving you energy to keep you going through the morning. Experiment with your favourite fruits and vegetables to find your ideal wake-me-up.

Serves 2

125 ml/4 fl oz/½ cup fat-free plain Greek yogurt

2 tbsp ground almonds

1 avocado, peeled, pitted and chopped

1 handful baby spinach leaves

squeeze of lemon juice

250 ml/8 fl oz/1 cup unsweetened almond or skimmed milk, or more to taste

a sprinkling of poppy seeds

Blend together all the ingredients except the poppy seeds until thick and creamy, adding a little extra milk if necessary. Serve sprinkled with poppy seeds.

Notes

All kinds of fruit and vegetables can go in your morning smoothie:

- Keep a peeled banana in the freezer for an instant thickener.
- Try skimmed milk, oat milk, unsweetened almond milk or other nut milks.
- A spoonful of fat-free plain Greek yogurt adds flavour and a creamy texture.
- Thicken with a spoonful of rolled oats.
- A shake of ground cinnamon adds sweetness as well as spice.
- Blending in a few chia seeds will thicken the smoothie.

OVERNIGHT OATS
with Chia & Peanut Butter

Soaking the oats in milk overnight gives a deliciously creamy and soft muesli-style breakfast. If you make it in individual jars, you can easily pop on the lid and have them ready at a moment's notice.

Serves 2

125 ml/4 fl oz/½ cup fat-free unsweetened Greek yogurt

200 ml/7 fl oz/¾ cup unsweetened almond or skimmed milk

50 g/2 oz/½ cup rolled oats

1 tbsp chia seeds

½ tsp vanilla extract

1 tbsp raw peanut butter (100 per cent peanuts)

1 handful blueberries

Mix together the yogurt, milk and oats, then stir in the chia seeds, vanilla and peanut butter until thoroughly blended. Spoon into individual jars and chill overnight in the refrigerator.

Top with blueberries to serve.

QUINOA PORRIDGE
with Raisins & Walnuts

Quinoa (pronounced 'keenwa') is a South American grain, high in protein and containing all nine essential amino acids, among other nutrients. You'll find it in all major supermarkets.

Serves 2

250 ml/8 fl oz/1 cup skimmed milk, plus extra to serve

250 ml/8 fl oz/1 cup water

175 g/6 oz/scant 1 cup quinoa

1 tsp dark soft brown sugar (optional)

1 tsp ground cinnamon

1 handful raisins or sultanas (golden raisins)

1 handful walnuts, roughly chopped

Bring the milk and water to the boil in a saucepan. Sprinkle in the quinoa, stirring, and return to the boil. Stir in the sugar, if using, then turn the heat down, cover and simmer for about 15 minutes until the quinoa is soft and the liquid has been absorbed. Remove from the heat.

Stir in the cinnamon, sprinkle with the raisins and walnuts and serve with a little milk poured over the top.

BUCKWHEAT PANCAKES WITH APPLES
& Nuts

If you don't have time to cook your own apple slices, buy a can of unsweetened apple slices or unsweetened apple sauce. Keep in an airtight container in the refrigerator and use within a few days once opened.

Serves 2

65 g/2½ oz/½ cup buckwheat flour

½ tsp ground cinnamon

½ tsp baking powder

1 egg, lightly beaten

½ tsp vanilla extract

150 ml/5 fl oz/⅔ cup oat or skimmed milk

oil spray (optional)

For the topping

2 tbsp walnut halves, whole almonds or other nuts

4 dessert apples, peeled, cored and chopped

To make the topping, toss the nuts in a dry pan over a medium heat until toasted, then chop.

Whisk together the flour, cinnamon, baking powder, egg, vanilla extract and most of the milk to a smooth, thick batter, adding all the milk if necessary.

Heat a nonstick frying pan and spray with a little oil, if you like. Add spoonfuls of the batter mixture so they spread into 8-cm/3¼-inch pancakes and cook for a few minutes until the bases are set and beginning to brown. Flip them over and fry the other side.

Meanwhile, put the apples in a small saucepan, rinse with water, then tip out the water, just leaving the drops on the apples. Heat gently, tossing occasionally, for a few minutes until warmed through and softening. Sprinkle the pancakes with the nuts and serve with the apple slices.

SHAKSHUKA

Coming from North Africa and the Middle East, this baked egg dish makes a delicious and hearty brunch. Use a glass-lidded pan, if you have one, so you can see when the eggs are just ready.

Serves 2-3

oil spray (optional)
1 onion, chopped
1 garlic clove, chopped
1 red pepper, deseeded and chopped
1 celery stalk, chopped
½ tsp paprika
½ tsp ground cumin
pinch chili powder
400 g/14 oz canned chopped tomatoes
3–4 eggs
freshly ground black pepper
2 tbsp chopped coriander (cilantro) leaves

Heat a nonstick pan and spray with a little oil, if you like. Add the onion, garlic, pepper and celery and cook on a low heat for a few minutes until softened but not browned, adding a little water if necessary. Stir in the paprika, cumin and chili and cook for 2 minutes. Stir in the tomatoes and simmer for 5–7 minutes until the sauce is reduced and quite thick.

Make three or four wells in the mixture. One at a time, break the eggs into a cup, then carefully pour them into the wells. Season with pepper and sprinkle with the coriander (cilantro). Cover and cook for a few minutes until the whites are set but the yolks still runny.

AVOCADO WITH POACHED EGGS
& Salsa

Serving the avocado with a fresh tomato salsa makes this a more substantial dish.

Serves 2

1 avocado

squeeze of lemon or 1 tsp lemon juice

2 small eggs

a few parsley leaves, chopped

pinch of cayenne or chili powder

freshly ground black pepper

For the tomato salsa (optional)

3 tbsp finely chopped onion

2 garlic cloves, crushed

3 large ripe tomatoes, seeded and chopped

1 fresh mild chili, seeded and chopped

2 tbsp chopped coriander (cilantro) leaves

1 tbsp lime juice, or to taste

freshly ground black pepper

If you are serving the salsa, simply mix all the ingredients together and leave to stand at room temperature for about an hour, if you have time, for the flavours to blend.

Halve the avocado and remove the pit. Scoop out a little more of the flesh to enlarge the holes so they are big enough for the eggs, then press the scooped-out flesh into the base of each cavity. Brush lightly with lemon juice.

Poach the eggs in gently simmering water for a couple of minutes or until cooked to your liking. Remove from the pan with a slotted spoon and place an egg in each avocado cavity. Sprinkle with the chopped parsley and cayenne or chili powder and a little grinding of pepper and serve with the tomato salsa, if using, while the eggs are still warm.

OMELETTE WITH MUSHROOM
& Feta Cheese

An omelette makes a tasty brunch dish, and you can make it more substantial by adding plenty of vegetables.

Serves 2

oil spray (optional)

2 spring onions (scallions), chopped

100 g/3½ oz button mushrooms

3 eggs

1 tbsp skimmed milk

freshly ground black pepper

2 tbsp crumbled feta cheese

a few parsley leaves

Heat a frying pan and lightly spray with oil, if you like. Add the spring onions (scallions) and fry over a low heat for 5 minutes until softened but not browned. Add the mushrooms and fry until they give up their moisture, then continue to fry until soft.

Whisk together the eggs and milk and season with pepper. Pour the mixture into the pan and allow to spread. Scatter the cheese over the top. Gently lift up the sides so the unset egg can run underneath, then continue to fry until the base is golden brown.

Fold the omelette in half and continue to cook over a low heat for a minute or so until only just set. Serve sprinkled with the parsley.

SALMON KEDGEREE

You can used leftover cooked salmon for this recipe, or use chicken or cooked prawns (shrimp) instead. In the case of smoked fish, only use a little as this is high in salt.

Serves 4

275 g /10 oz/1½ cups brown rice

1 litre/1¾ pints/4 cups homemade

(*see* page 183) or low-salt vegetable stock

2 eggs

225 g/8 oz salmon steak

4 tbsp unsweetened almond milk or skimmed milk

25 g/1 oz/2 tbsp/¼ stick unsalted butter

1 tbsp olive oil

1 onion, finely chopped

1 garlic clove, crushed

4 tbsp frozen peas

juice of 1 lime

½ tsp paprika

freshly ground black pepper

1 tbsp low-fat crème fraîche (optional)

Put the rice and stock in a saucepan and bring to the boil. Turn down the heat, cover and simmer for about 30 minutes until most of the stock has been absorbed and the rice is tender but with a little bite. Turn off the heat, keeping the lid on, and leave to stand for 10 minutes until the rice is perfectly tender and the stock absorbed. While the rice is cooking, put the eggs in a small saucepan and cover with water. Bring to the boil, then simmer for 8 minutes. Drain, then rinse in cold water. Once cool, peel the eggs and cut into quarters. Put the salmon steak in a saucepan with the milk, cover and cook over a low heat for about 8 minutes until the fish is cooked through and flakes easily when tested with a fork. Remove from the heat and leave to one side in the covered pan.

Melt the butter and oil in a wok or large frying pan, add the onion and garlic and fry over a low heat for about 5 minutes until softened but not browned. Add the peas, lime juice and paprika, then fold in the cooked rice and season with black pepper. Stir through the crème fraîche, if using. Gently fold in the chunks of fish and top with the eggs to serve.

SOUPS & SALADS

CHICKEN & MUSHROOM SOUP
with Coconut

This creamy soup has a Thai-style flavour with plenty of goodness from the vegetables. Remember to look for reduced-fat coconut milk.

Serves 4

400 g/14 oz can reduced-fat coconut milk

400 ml/14 fl oz/1⅔ cups homemade (*see* page 183) or low-salt chicken stock

2.5-cm/1-inch piece root ginger

1 lemongrass stalk

100 g/3½ oz button mushrooms, sliced

1 tbsp lime juice

1 tbsp fish sauce (nam pla)

1 tsp chili paste

1 tsp sugar (optional)

100 g/3½ oz cooked chicken, shredded

freshly ground black pepper

1 spring onion (scallion), trimmed and shredded

Put the coconut milk, stock, ginger and lemongrass in a saucepan and bring to the boil. Add the mushrooms, lime juice, fish sauce (nam pla), chili paste and sugar, if using, and cook for about 5 minutes until the mushrooms are tender.

Add the chicken, and season to taste with pepper. Discard the lemongrass and serve topped with the shredded spring onion (scallion).

CANNELLINI BEAN & TOMATO SOUP

For this recipe – a rich and wholesome soup with a bit of a kick – you can use any kind of pulse. Adjust the amount of chili you include to suit your own taste.

Serves 4

1 tbsp olive oil

1 onion, chopped

2 garlic cloves, chopped

2 carrots, chopped

1 small chili, deseeded and chopped

1 celery stalk, finely chopped

2 tbsp white wine

2 x 400 g/14 oz canned whole tomatoes

3 tbsp chopped coriander (cilantro) leaves

500 ml/18 fl oz/2 cups home-made (*see* page 183) or low-salt vegetable stock

freshly ground black pepper

dash of Tabasco sauce, optional

Heat the oil in a large saucepan and fry the onion, garlic, carrots, chili and celery for about 8 minutes until softened but not browned.

Add the wine and simmer for 1 minute, then add the tomatoes, most of the coriander (cilantro) leaves and stock. Bring to the boil, breaking up the tomatoes as you do so, then simmer for about 20 minutes until everything is soft and the flavours have blended. Season with pepper and a dash of Tabasco, if using. Ladle into warm bowls and sprinkle with the remaining coriander to garnish.

SWEET POTATO & RED LENTIL SOUP
with Ginger

Sweet potatoes have a lovely colour and texture and make a filling lunch that will help keep your blood sugar levels constant for several hours.

Serves 4

4 tbsp water

2 onions, finely chopped

1 garlic clove, chopped

1 celery stalk, finely chopped

1 dessert apple, peeled and chopped

2 large sweet potatoes, peeled and diced

2.5-cm/1-inch piece fresh root ginger, grated

2 tsp curry powder

175 g/6 oz/scant ¾ cup red lentils

1 litre/1¾ pints/4 cups homemade
  (*see* page 183) or low-salt vegetable stock

400 g/14 oz can reduced-fat
  coconut milk

3 tbsp chopped basil leaves,
  plus a few small leaves to
  garnish

juice of ½ lime

1 tbsp low-fat crème fraîche

freshly ground black pepper

Heat the water in a large pan and gently cook the onions, garlic and celery for about 5 minutes until softened but not browned. Add the apple, sweet potatoes and ginger and continue to cook for 5 minutes until softening and well blended.

Stir in the curry powder and cook for a minute or so. Add the lentils, stock and coconut milk, bring to the boil, then simmer for 20 minutes until the lentils and vegetables are tender. Add the chopped basil. Blitz with a stick blender, then season with lime juice and pepper to taste. Serve in warm mugs or bowls with a swirl of crème fraîche and a sprinkling of pepper and basil leaves.

BROCCOLI & WATERCRESS SOUP

As some people find watercress a bit too peppery, you don't have to use it – try it with other green vegetables instead. You could also use small onions instead of leeks.

Serves 4

1 tbsp olive oil

2 leeks, trimmed and finely chopped

2 garlic cloves, crushed

1 broccoli head, cut into florets, stem trimmed and chopped

4 medium potatoes, peeled and roughly chopped

100 g/3½ oz/3 cups watercress

1 litre/1¾ pints/4 cups homemade (*see* page 183) or low-salt vegetable stock

freshly ground black pepper

a squeeze of lemon juice (optional)

2 tbsp low-fat unsweetened crème fraîche

Heat the oil in a large saucepan and fry the leeks, garlic and broccoli stem for about 5 minutes until softened but not browned.

Add the potatoes, watercress and the remaining broccoli to the pan and stir all the ingredients together. Add the stock and bring to the boil, then simmer for about 20 minutes until all the vegetables are tender.

Blitz with a stick blender or in a food processor, then return to the pan. Heat through and season to taste with pepper and a little lemon juice, if using. Add a little boiling water if the soup is too thick. Serve with a swirl of crème fraîche.

ROAST BEETROOT SALAD
with Fig & Feta

Colourful and tasty, this nutritious salad combines sweet and savoury flavours, crisp and soft textures. You can serve it with or without the dressing.

Serves 4

1 red onion, thinly sliced

3 fresh figs, cut into wedges

100 g/3½ oz/½ cup cooked beetroot, trimmed and cut into wedges

125g/4 oz/4 cups baby spinach leaves

2 handfuls rocket leaves

125 g/4 oz/¾ cup feta, diced or crumbled

1 handful walnuts, roughly chopped

freshly ground black pepper

For the dressing

½ tbsp olive oil

2 tbsp red wine vinegar

2 tsp Dijon mustard

1 garlic clove, crushed

1 tsp chopped basil leaves

freshly ground black pepper

Simply mix together all the salad ingredients. Whisk together the dressing ingredients, pour a little over the salad and toss so the leaves are lightly coated.

THAI COURGETTE & PEANUT SALAD

Crisp and delicious, you can serve this salad on its own, with crusty wholegrain bread for a light lunch, or it goes well with a grilled (broiled) chicken breast or fish fillet.

Serves 4

50 g/2 oz/⅓ cup raw unsalted peanuts

450 g/1 lb courgettes (zucchini)

2 carrots, trimmed

1 onion, thinly sliced

For the dressing

3 tbsp lime juice

1 tbsp fish sauce (nam pla)

1 tbsp maple syrup

1 handful basil leaves

Toast the peanuts in a hot dry pan for a few minutes until browned and aromatic, shaking the pan occasionally. Remove from the pan and chop, then tip them into a bowl.

Cut a few fat ribbons of courgette (zucchini) using a potato peeler and put them in the bowl. Spiralize the remainder, or pare into ribbons, then cut into strips and add to the bowl. Spiralize or pare and cut the carrots into strips in the same way (but discard any thick ribbons). Add the onion. Toss all the ingredients together.

To make the dressing, mix the lime juice, fish sauce (nam pla) and maple syrup, then whisk until blended. Pour over the salad, toss together and finish with the basil leaves.

AVOCADO & BLOOD ORANGE SALAD
with Hazelnuts

Don't worry if you don't have blood oranges; ordinary oranges will do just as well. The dressing is optional but does add another flavour dimension.

Serves 4

50 g/2 oz/½ cup hazelnuts

350 g/12 oz/1¾ cups cooked quinoa

1 avocado

juice of ½ lemon

1 blood orange

1 passionfruit

3 tomatoes, cut into wedges

2 large handfuls baby spinach leaves

few small basil leaves

freshly ground black pepper

Light vinaigrette dressing (*see* page 182), to serve

Toss the hazelnuts in a dry pan over a medium heat until aromatic and browned. Tip out and leave to cool, then roughly chop.

Put the quinoa in a serving dish. Peel and pit the avocado and cut it into chunks, toss immediately in the lemon juice, then add to the dish. Cut the peel and pith off the orange, cut into segments and add to the dish. Cut the passionfruit in half and scrape most of the seeds into the dish. Add the tomatoes, spinach leaves, nuts and most of the basil, season with a little pepper and toss together gently.

Drizzle the dressing over the salad, toss again lightly, then serve sprinkled with the remaining passionfruit seeds and basil.

CHICKEN & BARLEY SALAD
with Pomegranate

Pomegranate molasses can be found in major supermarkets. Used sparingly, it gives a lovely sweet-sharp flavour to savoury and sweet dishes.

Serves 4

175 g/6 oz/generous ¾ cup pearl barley

1 handful sultanas (golden raisins)

1 bunch spring onions (scallions), chopped

100 g/3½ oz/⅔ cup unsalted pistachios, chopped

1 dessert apple, peeled, cored and chopped

100 g/3½ oz cooked chicken

2 pomegranates

1 handful crumbled feta

For the dressing

1 tbsp pomegranate molasses

1 tbsp olive oil

1 tsp lemon juice

½ tsp ground cinnamon

½ tsp ground cumin

freshly ground black pepper

Put the barley in a large saucepan and cover with water. Bring to the boil, then simmer for about 30 minutes until just tender. Drain well, then spread onto a baking (cookie) sheet and leave to cool completely.

When the barley is cool, tip it into a bowl and add the sultanas (golden raisins, spring onions (scallions), pistachios, apple and chicken and stir together well. Cut the pomegranates in half and scoop out the seeds into the salad, discarding any membranes. Sprinkle with the feta.

Whisk together the dressing ingredients, drizzle over the salad and toss together.

FISH & SEAFOOD

LIGURIAN FISH STEW

This simple, chunky fish stew is delicious made with any 'meaty', sustainable white fish. It is delicious with some olive ciabatta bread and wilted spinach.

Serves 4

1 tbsp olive oil

1 onion, halved and thinly sliced

2 garlic cloves, finely chopped

1 tsp cumin seeds

1 tsp fennel seeds

1 small fennel head, halved and sliced

2 pimientos from a jar, drained and cut into chunks

400 g/14 oz canned plum tomatoes

150 ml/¼ pint/⅔ cup dry white wine

450 g/1 lb chunky white fish, such as hake, skinned and cut into large cubes

freshly ground black pepper

1 tbsp chopped parsley leaves

olive ciabatta bread and wilted spinach, to serve

Heat the oil in a large saucepan. Add the onion and garlic and fry over a moderate heat, stirring, for 3 minutes until the onion is softened but not browned. Add the cumin and fennel seeds and fry for a further 30 seconds until fragrant.

Stir in the fennel, pimientos, tomatoes and wine. Break up the tomatoes with a wooden spoon. Bring to the boil, reduce the heat and simmer for 5 minutes until the fennel is almost tender. Add the fish and plenty of black pepper. Reduce the heat and simmer gently for 10 minutes until the fish is cooked through. Serve sprinkled with the chopped parsley, and with some olive ciabatta and wilted spinach.

SPICY FISH TACOS

These tacos make a delicious meal and you can use any sustainable white fish. Some are much more economical than cod or haddock, such as pollack, which we've used here. For added zip, stir a tablespoonful of chipotle paste into the crème fraîche.

Serves 4

8 small corn or wheat tortillas

2 tsp ground allspice

1 tsp ground turmeric

1 tsp smoked paprika

freshly ground black pepper

oil spray

450 g/1 lb pollack fillets, skinned and
    cut into bite-size cubes

1 lime

For the guacamole

1 large avocado

1 tsp lime juice

good pinch chili (hot pepper) flakes

To serve

shredded lettuce

sliced red onion

cherry tomatoes, quartered

low-fat crème fraîche

Heat a griddle pan and toast the tortillas for a few seconds each side until striped. Wrap in foil to keep warm until ready to serve. Mix the allspice, turmeric and paprika with plenty of black pepper. Pat the fish dry on a kitchen (paper) towel, then coat in the spice mix.

To make the guacamole, halve and pit the avocado, then scoop the flesh into a bowl, discarding the skin. Mash well with a fork, then mash in the lime juice and chili (hot pepper) flakes. Set aside.

Spray a nonstick frying pan with oil. When hot, add the fish and fry, turning gently until cooked through. Halve the lime and squeeze the juice over the fish.

Fill each taco shell with the shredded lettuce, onion and tomato, add cubes of fish, a dollop of guacamole and a dollop of crème fraîche. Use fingers to eat.

MACKEREL IN OATMEAL
with Warm White Beans

Mackerel is an oily fish containing plenty of valuable omega 3 fatty acids. You can include it a couple of times a week in your meal planning.

Serves 4

8 tbsp pinhead (steel-cut) oatmeal

2 tbsp finely chopped parsley leaves,
   plus extra to garnish

1 tbsp picked thyme leaves, finely chopped

freshly ground black pepper

1 egg, beaten

4 large or 6 small mackerel fillets

oil spray

400 g/14 oz canned cannellini (white kidney)
   beans, drained and rinsed

1 garlic clove, crushed

1 little gem lettuce, separated into leaves

1 small red bell pepper, deseeded and sliced

¼ cucumber, diced

lemon wedges, to garnish

For the salsa

2 tbsp olive oil

2 celery stalks, chopped

1 small onion, chopped

1 garlic clove, crushed

2 tomatoes, skinned and chopped

juice of 1 lemon

2 tbsp water

To prepare the salsa, heat the oil in a small pan and fry the celery, onion and garlic over a gentle heat, stirring occasionally, for 5 minutes until softened but not browned. Add the tomatoes, lemon juice and water. Heat through just before serving.

Mix the oatmeal with the herbs and plenty of pepper in a shallow dish. Beat the egg in a separate dish. Check the mackerel fillets and remove any bones with tweezers. Dip the fish first in the egg, then in the oatmeal mixture to coat. Spray a large nonstick frying pan with oil and heat through. Add the mackerel fillets and fry for 3–4 minutes each side until golden brown, adding a little more oil spray if necessary. Transfer to a plate and keep warm.

Wipe out the frying pan with kitchen (paper) towels. Add the beans and their liquid, the garlic and a little more pepper. Heat through, stirring.

Arrange the lettuce leaves on serving plates. Cut the fish into chunky pieces and scatter over the top. Drain the beans and scatter them over the fish with the pepper slices and cucumber. Sprinkle with the remaining chopped parsley and garnish with lemon wedges. Serve with the warmed salsa.

SWEET POTATO-TOPPED FISH PIE

This delicious fish pie can be made with all white fish, cut in chunks, but with the sweet potato topping, the combination of flavours when using a fish pie mix is irresistible. A little bit of smoked fish, although higher in salt, is fine in a balanced diet.

Serves 4

700 g/1½ lb sweet potatoes, peeled and cut into even-size chunks

1 small head broccoli, cut into small florets

1 courgette (zucchini), sliced

100g/3½ oz/⅔ cup frozen peas

25 g/1oz/2 tbsp/¼ stick butter

300 ml/½ pint/1¼ cups skimmed milk plus 2 tbsp

freshly ground black pepper

1 onion, chopped

1 bay leaf

¼ tsp freshly grated nutmeg

400 g/14 oz fish pie mix or all white fish

2 tbsp plain (all-purpose) flour

Put the sweet potatoes in a pan, just cover with water and bring to the boil. Put the broccoli, courgette (zucchini) and peas in a steamer or large metal colander over the pan, cover and steam for 5 minutes until just tender. Remove the steamer from the pan. Continue to cook the sweet potatoes for a further 15 minutes or so, depending on size, until really tender. Drain thoroughly, then return to the pan. Add half the butter and the 2 tablespoons of the milk and mash well. Season with pepper. Set aside.

Meanwhile, melt the remaining butter in a saucepan. Add the onion and cook gently for 3 minutes, stirring until softening. Add all but 2 tablespoons of the remaining milk, the bay leaf, nutmeg and some pepper. Bring to the boil, reduce the heat, cover and simmer gently for 5 minutes. Add the fish, re-cover and cook gently for about 3 minutes until just cooked through. Carefully lift the fish out of the pan with a slotted spoon and place in four individual flameproof dishes. Add the cooked broccoli, courgette and peas.

Blend the flour with the remaining milk. Stir into the milk left from cooking the fish. Bring to the boil, then cook for 2 minutes, stirring. Discard the bay leaf. Taste and add more pepper, if you like. Pour over the fish and vegetables. Top with the sweet potato mash and rough up with a fork. Place under a preheated grill (broiler) and cook until golden brown and bubbling. Serve hot.

PRAWN STIR-FRY WITH BROCCOLI

Juicy tiger prawns tossed quickly with broccoli, red onion, red pepper, garlic, chili and coriander (cilantro) make a delicious quick meal. Try it with wholewheat egg noodles that take only minutes to cook.

Serves 4

1 tbsp sunflower oil

1 red onion, halved and thinly sliced

1 large garlic clove, crushed

1 red pepper, deseeded and thinly sliced

1 head broccoli, cut into tiny florets

2 tsp grated fresh root ginger

1 lemongrass stalk, trimmed and finely chopped

1 fat red chili, deseeded and finely chopped

400 g/14 oz raw, peeled tiger prawns (shrimp)

splash of fish sauce (nam pla), to taste

good squeeze of lime juice

1 tbsp torn coriander (cilantro) leaves

2 nests wholewheat egg noodles, 1 tsp toasted sesame oil, to serve (optional)

Heat the oil in a wok. Add the onion, garlic, pepper and broccoli and stir-fry over a moderate heat for 3 minutes until softening but still with plenty of bite. Add the ginger, lemongrass, chili and prawns (shrimp) and stir-fry for a further 3 minutes until the prawns are pink. Add the fish sauce, a good squeeze of lime juice and the coriander (cilantro) and toss gently. Taste and adjust the seasoning with more fish sauce or lime juice as needed.

Meanwhile, if serving the noodles, cook them according to the packet instructions, stirring well during cooking to separate. Drain, toss with the sesame oil, then serve with the stir-fry.

SESAME SALMON SKEWERS
with Courgette & Tomato Salad

These can be prepared well in advance. The white balsamic gives a slightly sweet and sour flavour which is good served with brown rice tossed with a little reduced-salt soy sauce and a sprinkling of five-spice powder.

Serves 4

4 small salmon tail fillets

2 tbsp reduced-salt soy sauce

1 tbsp water

1 tbsp toasted sesame oil

1 tbsp grated fresh root ginger

1 tsp Chinese five-spice powder

1 garlic clove, crushed

1 tbsp white balsamic condiment

1 tbsp mirin (Japanese rice wine)

1 tbsp sesame seeds

4 wooden skewers, soaked in cold water

For the salad

2 courgettes (zucchini)

12 cherry tomatoes, halved

2 tbsp rice wine vinegar

1 tbsp mirin

white part of a spring onion (scallion),
    trimmed and very finely chopped

Cut the salmon fillets in half lengthways and lay in a single layer in a large, nonmetallic baking dish. Combine the remaining ingredients and brush over the fish. Marinate for at least an hour.

To prepare the salad, pare the courgettes (zucchini) into ribbons with a potato peeler. Gently toss in a bowl with the tomatoes, rice wine vinegar, mirin and spring onion (scallion). Chill.

When nearly ready to cook, preheat a grill (broiler). Thread 2 fish fillets concertina-style on each skewer. Place on the grill rack and cook close to the heat for about 3 minutes each side until golden and cooked through, brushing with any marinade left in the dish during cooking. Serve the skewers with the salad alongside.

POULTRY & MEAT

LEMON CHICKEN WITH OLIVES

If you don't like olives you can use button mushrooms instead, but the flavour won't be so intense. If you want a change from couscous, try cooking quinoa.

Serves 4

2 lemons

oil spray

8 small skinless chicken thighs

1 onion, halved and thinly sliced

1 large garlic clove, crushed

1 tsp ground cumin

1½ tsp ground cinnamon

1 tbsp sweet paprika

400 ml/14 fl oz/1⅔ cups low-salt chicken stock

2 tbsp raisins

50 g/2 oz/⅓ cup large pitted black olives

freshly ground black pepper

couscous and green beans, to serve

Preheat the oven to 180°C/350°F/Gas 4.

Cut 1 lemon into thin slices. Grate the zest and squeeze the juice from the second. Set aside.

Heat a nonstick frying pan and spray lightly with oil. Brown the chicken thighs on all sides, then remove from the pan and place in a casserole dish. Add the onion to the pan and fry, stirring, for 2–3 minutes until lightly golden brown. Add the garlic and spices and fry for a further 30 seconds. Stir in the stock, lemon zest and juice and the raisins. Pour over the chicken and add the olives and a good grinding of pepper. Scatter the lemon slices over, cover and cook in the oven for 1 hour.

Serve hot with couscous and green beans.

SMOKY CHICKEN SKEWERS

Marinate these well so the flavour penetrates the flesh, or try with turkey; or barbecue instead of using the grill (broiler). You could also serve them with long-grain brown rice, cooked in tasty stock.

Serves 4–6

2 tbsp olive oil

5 tbsp medium white wine

2 garlic cloves, finely chopped

4 tsp chipotle (smoked chili) paste

½ tsp dried oregano

1 tbsp chopped parsley leaves

freshly ground black pepper

2–3 large, skinless chicken breasts

For the salad

12 cherry tomatoes, halved

¼ cucumber, diced

1 carrot, cut into fine matchsticks

½ papaya, deseeded, peeled and
   cut into pieces

1 handful fresh basil leaves, torn

2 tbsp white balsamic condiment

Put the oil, wine, garlic, chipotle (smoked chili) paste, oregano, parsley and plenty of pepper in a large, shallow dish and whisk together. Cut each chicken breast into bite-size chunks. Add to the marinade and toss together well. Cover and leave to marinate in the refrigerator for 2 hours, if possible.

Meanwhile, put all the salad ingredients in a bowl and toss together well. Chill until ready to serve.

Preheat the grill (broiler). Thread the chicken onto kebab skewers. Place on foil on the grill rack as close as possible to the heat source and cook for 3–4 minutes on each side until cooked through and well browned in places, brushing with any remaining marinade during cooking. Serve straightaway with the salad.

CREAMY TURMERIC CHICKEN
with Mushrooms

Chicken and mushrooms in a creamy tahini-enhanced sauce on a bed of brown rice makes a wholesome meal. Instead of rice you could add a 400g/14 oz can of drained butter (lima) beans to the stew.

Serves 4

200 g/7 oz/1 cup long-grain brown rice

2 tsp olive oil

1 onion, chopped

2 garlic cloves, crushed

1 tsp ground turmeric1 tsp ground cumin

½ tsp chili (hot pepper) flakes

3 star anise

750 ml/1¼ pint/3¼ cups homemade vegetable (see page 183)
   or low-salt vegetable or chicken stock

1 red pepper, deseeded and chopped

100 g/3½ oz button mushrooms, sliced

1 bay leaf

4 small, skinless chicken breasts

freshly ground black pepper

2 tbsp tahini

4 tbsp low-fat crème fraîche

a few chopped basil or parsley leaves, to garnish

crisp green salad, including some avocado, to serve

Cook the rice in plenty of boiling water for about 20 minutes until just tender but still with some bite. Drain in a colander and keep warm over the pan with a little hot water in it. Meanwhile, heat the oil in a saucepan. Add the onion and garlic and fry, stirring, for

2 minutes until softened but not browned. Add the spices and fry for a further 30 seconds, stirring. Add the stock, pepper, mushrooms, bay leaf and the whole chicken breasts. Sprinkle with a good grinding of black pepper. Bring to the boil, then reduce the heat, part-cover and simmer gently for about 15 minutes, or until the chicken is tender and cooked through.

Lift the chicken out of the pan with some of the mushrooms and pepper and cut the meat into thick slices. Discard the star anise and bay leaf. Stir in the tahini, then the crème fraîche. Do not allow to boil again. Taste and add more pepper if necessary.

Spoon the rice into four warm serving bowls. Spoon over the tahini sauce, then pile the chicken and mushrooms in the bowls. Sprinkle with a little chopped basil or parsley and serve hot with a crisp green salad, including some avocado.

DUCK WITH MINTED CHICKPEA
& Carrot Patties with Orange Sauce

This is a great way to make two large duck breasts serve four, either threading the cooked duck onto skewers or thinly slicing to serve with patties and a dipping sauce. The crispy skin is a real treat, but remove before serving if you prefer.

Serves 4

2 large, skin-on duck breasts
freshly ground black pepper

For the chickpea patties

400 g/14 oz canned chickpeas (garbanzo beans), drained
1 shallot, quartered
1 garlic clove, roughly chopped
½ tsp ground cinnamon
1 handful mint sprigs, leaves picked, plus a few sprigs, to garnish
freshly ground black pepper
50 g/2 oz/scant ½ cup chickpea (gram) flour, plus extra for dusting
3 tbsp sunflower or rapeseed oil

For the sauce

2 large oranges
65 ml/2½ fl oz/¼ cup homemade vegetable (*see* page 183)
   or low-salt vegetable or chicken stock
1 tbsp tomato purée (paste)
1 tsp cornflour (cornstarch)
1 tbsp water

To serve

4 wooden skewers

a peppery watercress and cucumber salad, dressed with
   a little vinaigrette (*see* page 182)

To make the patties, put the chickpeas, shallot, garlic and cinnamon in a food processor. Reserve 6 mint leaves for the sauce and add the rest to the processor with a good grinding of pepper, then blitz until the mixture is well chopped, stopping and scraping down the sides as necessary. Remove the blade and work in the gram flour to form a dough. Shape into 16 small balls, then roll out on a lightly floured surface into 8 thin patties. Chill.

To make the sauce, finely grate the zest of one orange and squeeze the juice. Cut off all the rind and pith from the second one and, holding the orange over a bowl, separate into segments either side of the membranes, adding the fruit to the pan. Squeeze the membranes over the pan to extract the last of the juice. Stir in the stock and tomato purée. Chop the reserved mint and add. Blend the cornflour (cornstarch) with the water and stir in. Bring to the boil, stirring until thickened and clear. Cover with a circle of wet baking parchment to prevent a skin forming.

Season the duck skins with pepper. Heat a nonstick frying pan and place the duck skin-side down in the pan. Heat fairly gently until the fat runs, then turn up the heat and fry for about 4 minutes until crisp and golden. Turn the duck over and cook for a further 3–6 minutes (for pink to well done). Remove from the pan and drain well on a kitchen (paper) towel, then wrap in foil to rest while you cook the remaining patties.

Heat half the oil in a large, nonstick frying pan. Add half the patties and fry for a couple of minutes on each side until crisp and golden. Drain on a kitchen towel. Cook the remaining patties.

To serve, cut 5-mm/¼-inch diagonal slices from the duck breasts and, if desired, thread the strips concertina fashion onto the skewers. Garnish with mint sprigs and serve with the patties, sauce and a watercress and cucumber salad.

TURKEY MEATBALLS
in Rich Tomato Sauce

Serve this simple midweek treat with pasta, ideally one with added fibre, and cook it *al dente* so it doesn't raise your blood sugar levels too much.

Serves 4

1 large onion, quartered

2 garlic cloves

20 sage leaves

oil spray

400 g/14 oz minced (ground) turkey

2 tbsp rolled oats

2 tbsp freshly grated Parmesan

1 small egg, beaten

freshly ground black pepper

400 g/14 oz canned chopped tomatoes

1 bay leaf

1 tbsp tomato purée (paste)

3 tbsp red wine

spaghetti with added fibre and a crisp
 green salad, to serve

Purée the onion, garlic and sage, stopping and scraping down the sides as necessary. Spray a frying pan with oil. Fry the onion mixture gently, stirring, for about 3 minutes until fragrant but not brown. Remove from the heat. Spoon half the mixture into a mixing bowl. Add the turkey, oats, Parmesan, the egg and a good grinding of pepper and mix well. Shape the mixture into about 20 small balls.

Add the tomatoes to the remaining onion mixture in the frying pan. Stir in the bay leaf, tomato purée (paste) and wine and add a good grinding of pepper. Bring to the boil, reduce the heat and simmer for 5 minutes until thickened and pulpy. Discard the bay leaf.

Meanwhile, heat a separate frying pan and spray with oil. Add the turkey balls and fry for a few minutes until browned on all sides and cooked through. Add to the tomato sauce and simmer for a few minutes, turning until they are bathed in the rich, thick sauce. Serve with spaghetti and a crisp green salad.

LAMB & PRUNE TAGINE

This tender lamb casserole is slow-cooked in a sauce rich with earthy prunes and the warmth of ginger, cinnamon and cumin. In the couscous, you could use peas or chopped green beans instead of the peppers.

Serves 4

700g/1½ lb lean stewing lamb, diced

1½ tsp ground cinnamon

1 tsp ground ginger

1 tsp ground cumin

1 garlic clove, crushed

freshly ground black pepper

1 tbsp olive oil

1 onion, chopped

125 g/4 oz/1 cup ready-to-eat pitted prunes

1 tomato, finely chopped

600ml/1 pint/2½ cups homemade (*see* page 183) or low-salt lamb or vegetable stock, plus extra to cook the couscous (optional)

2 tbsp tomato purée (paste)

a few coriander (cilantro) leaves

1 tbsp flaked (slivered) almonds, to garnish

For the couscous

225 g/8 oz/1¼ cups giant couscous

1 small red pepper, deseeded and finely chopped

1 small yellow pepper, deseeded and finely chopped

Use your hands to mix the meat thoroughly with the spices, garlic and plenty of black pepper. Heat the oil in a flameproof casserole dish and fry the onion for 2 minutes, stirring until softened. Add the meat and continue to fry for several minutes, turning until browned all over. Add all the remaining ingredients except the garnish. Bring to the boil, reduce the heat, part-cover and simmer gently for 1½–2 hours until the meat is really tender, stirring occasionally.

When nearly ready to serve, cook the couscous according to the packet instructions, adding the peppers with the stock or water. Drain, tip into a serving bowl and fluff with a fork. Garnish with the torn coriander (cilantro) and flaked (slivered) almonds. Serve with the couscous.

GINGER BEEF NOODLES

Stir-fried steak strips are a tender and budget-friendly alternative to rump or fillet (filet mignon) steak. Ring the changes with carrot, cucumber, celery stalks or sliced mushrooms.

Serves 4

2–4 nests of wholewheat egg noodles

2 tbsp sunflower oil

350 g/12 oz beef stir-fry strips

4 spring onions (scallions), sliced

1 large garlic clove, crushed

1 red pepper, deseeded and cut into strips

1 yellow pepper, deseeded and cut into strips

1 red chili, deseeded and finely chopped (optional)

100 g/3½ oz green beans, trimmed and cut into short lengths

1 tbsp grated fresh root ginger

3 tbsp reduced-salt soy sauce

4 tbsp water

1 tsp clear honey

a few flat-leaf parsley or coriander (cilantro) leaves, to garnish

Cook the noodles according to the packet instructions. Drain and set aside.

Heat half the oil in a wok, add the beef and stir-fry for 2 minutes. Remove from the pan with a slotted spoon and set aside. Add the remaining oil to the pan and stir-fry the spring onions (scallions), garlic, peppers, chili and green beans for several minutes until softened to your liking. Return the beef to the pan and add the ginger, soy sauce, water and honey. Stir-fry a few minutes more. Stir in the drained noodles and toss until they are coated in the sauce and well mixed in. Garnish with a few parsley or coriander (cilantro) leaves and serve hot.

GRILLED PORK WITH SALSA VERDE

Pork fillet (tenderloin) is lean and tender so takes very little cooking. Here it is served with a vibrant sauce and some griddled vegetables. It also goes well with sweet potato fries (see page 172) and/or Chantenay carrots.

Serves 4

1 large pork fillet (tenderloin),
    cut into 4 pieces
2 tsp olive oil
freshly ground black pepper
½ tsp chili (hot pepper) flakes
oil spray
1 large courgette (zucchini), sliced
1 small aubergine (eggplant), sliced

For the salsa verde

6 anchovy fillets, chopped
2 tsp brined capers, drained and chopped
1 garlic clove, crushed
finely grated zest and juice of 1 lime
1 handful basil leaves, chopped, plus extra to garnish
1 handful flat-leaf parsley, chopped
1 handful mint, chopped
2 tbsp olive oil
4 tsp white balsamic condiment
1 tsp Dijon mustard

First make the salsa verde. Mix all the ingredients together and leave to stand to allow the flavours to blend. Then trim any membranes from the pork. Rub with the oil and sprinkle with the black pepper and chili (hot pepper) flakes. Heat a nonstick frying pan and add the pork. Cover with a heatproof plate and weigh down with cans of food to flatten the pork. Cook for about 5 minutes each side until browned. Wrap in foil and leave to rest for 5 minutes.

Heat a griddle pan and spray with oil. Fry the courgette (zucchini) and aubergine (eggplant) a few slices at a time until tender, turning once. Keep warm while you cook the remainder.

Place the pork on serving plates, pouring any juices into the salsa verde. Spoon a little salsa verde over the pork, then cut into thick slices. Garnish with the basil and serve with the griddled vegetables and the remaining sauce.

MEAT-FREE MAIN COURSES

MUSHROOM BARLEY RISOTTO

Non veggies might want to add some pieces of lean chicken breast to this dish. Using barley instead of the traditional rice makes it lower GI. For added richness, stir in about 3 tablespoons reduced-fat crème fraîche before serving.

Serves 4

2 tsp olive oil

1 onion, finely chopped1 garlic clove, peeled and crushed

400 g/12 oz mixed wild and chestnut (cremini) mushrooms

200 ml/7 fl oz/¾ cup dry white wine

300 g/10½ oz/scant ½ cup pearl barley

2 tsp fresh thyme leaves, plus small sprigs to garnish

1 litre/1¾ pts/1 quart homemade (*see* page 183) or low-salt vegetable
   or chicken stock

2 tbsp freshly grated Parmesan

freshly ground black pepper

salad or a green vegetable, to serve

Heat the oil in a large frying pan and fry the onion and garlic over a low heat for a few minutes until softened but not browned. Add the mushrooms and wine and simmer for a couple of minutes. Add the barley and thyme and stir everything together.

Add the stock, bring to the boil, then simmer gently for about 40 minutes until the barley is tender and most of the liquid has been absorbed. Stir in half the Parmesan and season to taste with pepper. Sprinkle the remaining Parmesan over the top and serve with salad or a green vegetable.

CAULIFLOWER DHANSAK

You can use cauliflower rice – simply cauliflower blitzed in a food processor – as a low-carb alternative to rice in any dish. Steam or boil in water or stock for a few minutes.

Serves 4

2 tsp olive oil

1 onion, finely chopped

2 garlic cloves, peeled and crushed

5-cm/2-inch piece fresh root ginger, grated

1 tsp ground cumin

1 tsp dried chili (hot pepper) flakes

2 tsp garam masala

1½ tsp ground cardamom

250 g/9 oz/1 cup red lentils

12 cherry tomatoes

400 g/14 oz canned chopped tomatoes

300 ml/½ pint/1¼ cups homemade (see page 183) or low-salt vegetable stock

1 cauliflower, cut into florets

1–2 handfuls baby spinach leaves, shredded

freshly ground black pepper

wholemeal (whole grain) naan bread or basmati rice, to serve

Heat the oil in a large pan and fry the onion, garlic and ginger for a few minutes until softened but not browned. Stir in the cumin, chili, garam masala and cardamom and fry, stirring, until the spices are well blended and aromatic.

Stir in the lentils, cherry tomatoes and canned tomatoes, then the stock, bring to the boil, then simmer gently for about 20 minutes until the lentils are tender. Some lentils may take a bit longer, in which case you may need to add a little water.

Meanwhile, pulse the cauliflower in a food processor until it looks like rice. Stir it into the pan, then simmer for a few minutes until tender and the stock has been absorbed.

Stir though the spinach until it wilts. Season with pepper and serve with naan bread or basmati rice.

ASPARAGUS & BROCCOLI TART

You could make this pastry shell with a single sheet of reduced-fat puff pastry if you prefer.

Serves 4

oil spray

250 g/9 oz packet filo pastry

1 small broccoli head,
  cut into small florets

8 asparagus tips

1 courgette (zucchini), thinly sliced

3 tbsp low-fat crème fraîche

2 tsp pesto, homemade (*see* page 181)
  or store bought

100 g/3½ oz/⅔ cups feta, crumbled

mixed leaf salad with rocket

1 handful mint leaves

freshly ground black pepper

tomato and onion salad with olives, to serve

Preheat the oven to 200°C/400°F/Gas 6 and lightly spray a 20-cm/8-inch round pie pan with oil. Lay a sheet of filo pastry into the pan, overlapping the edges, then spray with a little oil. Add another layer and spray lightly with oil, then continue in this way until you have used all the pastry. Shape and roughly crimp the edges and bake in the oven for about 15 minutes until the pastry is crisp and golden.

Meanwhile, bring a large pan of water to the boil, add the broccoli and boil for 2 minutes, then add the asparagus and boil for 1 minute, then finally the courgette (zucchini) and boil for a further 1–2 minutes until the vegetables are only just tender but still crunchy. Drain.

Remove the pastry case from the oven and carefully transfer to a serving plate. Mix together the crème fraîche and pesto and spoon into the base of the case. Drain the vegetables and spoon on top. Sprinkle with the feta, pile on the salad, the mint leaves and season with a generous grinding of pepper.

Serve with a tomato and onion salad garnished with a few olives.

TOFU SATAY LETTUCE WRAPS

Lettuce leaves make surprisingly good wraps instead of the traditional kind, and keep your carb count down.

Serves 4

1 tsp sesame oil

6 spring onions (scallions) thinly sliced

2.5-cm/1-inch piece fresh root ginger, grated

2 carrots, diced

4 radishes, thinly sliced

400 g/14 oz/1⅔ cups firm tofu, drained and diced

4 tbsp finely chopped coriander (cilantro) leaves

3 tbsp reduced-salt soy sauce

1 tsp hot pepper sauce, or to taste

1 handful button mushrooms

freshly ground black pepper

4 large lettuce leaves

1 small handful raw peanuts

For the peanut sauce

oil spray

2 garlic cloves, crushed

2 shallots, finely chopped

150 ml/¼ pint/⅔ cup water

2 tbsp raw peanut butter (100 per cent peanuts)

1 tbsp hoisin sauce

2 tsp lime juice

pinch of chili (hot pepper) flakes, or to taste

freshly ground black pepper

To make the sauce, spray a nonstick frying pan with oil spray. Add the garlic and shallots and fry over a low heat for a few minutes until softened but not browned, adding a little of the water if the mixture begins to stick. Mix the remaining water with the peanut butter to loosen it, then stir in the hoisin sauce, lime juice and chili (hot pepper) flakes. Stir into the pan and mix until well blended. Purée with a stick blender for a smooth sauce. Season with pepper.

For the tofu, heat the sesame oil in a nonstick pan and fry the spring onions (scallions), ginger and carrots for a few minutes until soft. Add the radishes and tofu and toss in the flavoured oil. Add half the coriander (cilantro), the soy sauce and hot pepper sauce and stir together well. Add the mushrooms and season with pepper. Stir together over a medium heat for a few minutes until hot but still crunchy.

Spoon the mixture into the lettuce leaves, sprinkle with the peanuts and serve with the sauce.

RICOTTA-STUFFED COURGETTES

For quicker preparation, simply slice the courgettes (zucchini) into thick chunks and hollow out the centres. Chop the flesh and mix it into the sauce. Be judicious with your use of tomato purée (paste); it is a useful flavour enhancer but does contain added salt.

Serves 4

4 courgettes (zucchini)

250 g/9 oz/1 cup ricotta, crumbled

1 tsp grated lemon zest

2 small carrots, grated

1 tsp chili (hot pepper) flakes

1 tbsp chopped basil leaves

50 g/2 oz/½ cup Parmesan, freshly grated

crisp green salad, to serve

For the tomato sauce

1 tsp olive oil

1 onion, finely chopped

1 celery stalk, finely chopped

1 garlic clove, crushd

1 carrot, finely chopped

400 g/14 oz canned chopped tomatoes

1 tbsp tomato purée (paste) (optional)

1 tsp fennel seeds (optional)

freshly ground black pepper

Preheat the oven to 200°C/400°F/Gas 6.

To start the sauce, heat the oil in a large, ovenproof, flameproof pan and fry the onion, celery, garlic and carrot for several minutes until softened but not browned. Add the tomatoes and tomato purée (paste) and fennel seeds, if using. Simmer gently for 15 minutes or so until thick and pulpy, stirring occasionally. Season to taste with black pepper.

Meanwhile, cut the courgettes (zucchini) lengthways into thin, flat ribbons using a vegetable peeler or a mandolin. Chop any small pieces finely and add them to the tomato sauce. Blitz the sauce with a stick blender for a smooth sauce, or leave it chunky.

Mix together the ricotta, lemon zest, carrots, chili (hot pepper) flakes and basil. Place a spoonful on a couple of overlapping slices of courgette, roll it up around the filling and secure with cocktail sticks (toothpicks). Continue until you have used all the ingredients. Sit the courgette rolls in the sauce, sprinkle with Parmesan and bake for about 20 minutes until golden.

Serve with a crisp green salad.

AUBERGINE & TOMATO LAYER

A tasty bake to serve on its own or with some couscous and cooked green beans.
Try them cold, tossed in a little chopped shallot, olive oil and red wine vinegar.

Serves 4

1 tsp olive oil

1 onion, chopped

2 garlic cloves, crushed

1 celery stalk, finely chopped

1 green pepper, deseeded and finely chopped

400 g/14 oz canned chopped tomatoes

1 tsp dried oregano

freshly ground black pepper

1 aubergine (eggplant), very thinly sliced on a mandolin

125 g/4 oz mozzarella, torn into pieces

a few basil leaves, torn

roasted or green vegetables or a green salad, to serve

Heat the oil in a frying pan and fry the onion, garlic, celery and pepper for a few
minutes until softened but not browned. Stir in the tomatoes and oregano and simmer
for about 10 minutes until the sauce begins to thicken. Season with pepper.

Meanwhile, place the aubergine (eggplant) slices in a steamer and steam over boiling
water for about 5 minutes until tender.

Layer the aubergine slices and the tomato sauce in a small casserole dish. Scatter
the mozzarella over the top and grill (broil) until the cheese is melted. Sprinkle with the
basil leaves and serve warm with roasted or green vegetables or a green salad.

SUMMER PASTA WITH BEANS

If you can buy fresh broad (fava) beans – or grow your own – that's great, but frozen beans are equally nutritious and a lot less work. You can use wholemeal or ordinary pasta but cook until just *al dente*, not soft, for low GI (*see* page 46).

Serves 4

400 g/14 oz farfalle or other pasta shapes,
  preferably wholemeal or with added fibre
400 g/14 oz/2½ cups frozen broad
  (fava) beans
1 yellow pepper, deseeded and diced
4 ripe tomatoes, cut into chunks
1 small handful chives, snipped
1 thyme sprig, leaves picked
freshly ground black pepper

For the dressing

1 tsp olive oil
1 shallot
1 garlic clove, crushed
120 ml/4 fl oz/½ cup cider vinegar
1 tsp clear honey
2 tbsp reduced-salt tomato purée (paste)

Bring a large pan of water to the boil, add the pasta and boil for about 8 minutes until only just tender (it needs to have some bite to slow absorption). Drain well. Meanwhile bring a second pan of water to the boil, add the broad (fava) beans and cook for about 3 minutes until just tender.

While they are cooking, heat the oil for the dressing and fry the shallot and garlic for a few minutes until soft but not browned. Stir in the vinegar, honey and tomato purée (paste) and heat through, stirring until well blended.

Drain the pasta and beans, then tip them into a bowl, add the pepper and tomatoes and toss together well. Drizzle with the warm dressing, sprinkle with chives and thyme leaves. Season with pepper to taste.

SIDES & SAUCES

TABOULEH

This delicious salad is perfect for a light lunch with crumbled feta cheese, grilled meat, chicken or fish.

Serves 4

125 g/4 oz/¾ cup bulgur wheat

300 ml/½ pint/1¼ cups boiling homemade (*see* page 183) or low-salt vegetable stock

1 small bunch coriander (cilantro), chopped

1 small bunch mint, leaves picked and chopped

1 large bunch parsley, chopped

4 tomatoes, finely chopped

1 small red onion, finely chopped

1 tbsp lemon juice, plus extra if needed

2 tbsp olive oil

freshly ground black pepper

lemon wedges, to garnish

Put the bulgur in a bowl and stir in the boiling stock. Leave to stand for 20–30 minutes until swollen and all the liquid has been absorbed. Stir in the herbs and leave to cool.

When nearly ready to serve, mix in the tomatoes and onion and moisten with the lemon juice and oil. Season to taste with pepper and add more lemon juice, if you like. Spoon into serving bowls and garnish each one with a wedge of lemon.

ROASTED TURMERIC CAULIFLOWER

This is the perfect accompaniment to any curry. It also makes a really tasty starter.

Serves 4

2 tsp sunflower or rapeseed (canola) oil

6 tbsp water

1 tbsp ground turmeric

1 tbsp cumin seeds

1 large garlic clove, crushed

1 small cauliflower, cut into small florets

To garnish

fat-free plain Greek yogurt

fennel or dill sprigs

flat-leaf parsley sprigs

lemon wedges

Preheat the oven to 230°C/450°F/Gas 8.

Whisk the oil with half the water, the turmeric, half the cumin seeds and the garlic in a large bowl. Add the cauliflower florets and toss until well coated.

Line a baking (cookie) sheet with baking parchment. Spread out the cauliflower florets on the paper. Spoon over the remaining water. Bake in the oven for about 20 minutes until tender and well-browned in places.

Meanwhile, toast the remaining cumin seeds in a hot pan for a few seconds until fragrant. Tip onto a saucer so they don't continue to cook. When ready to serve, spoon some yogurt on four serving plates. Top with the cauliflower, sprinkle the toasted cumin seeds over the top and garnish with the herbs and lemon wedges.

RED LENTIL DHAL

Dhal makes a quick, nutritious curry that you can serve with raw onion and lemon wedges as a simple meal or to accompany any meat, poultry, fish or vegetable curry, or even grilled marinated paneer or the turmeric cauliflower on page 169.

Serves 4

175 g/6 oz/scant ¾ cup red lentils

1 garlic clove, crushed

1 tsp ground turmeric

1 tsp grated fresh root ginger

500 ml/18 fl oz/2 cups homemade
   (*see* page 183) or low-salt chicken
   or vegetable stock, or water

1 tbsp sunflower oil

1 onion, finely chopped

1 tsp ground cumin

1 tsp ground coriander

2 tsp sweet paprika

1 tsp crushed chili (hot pepper) flakes

1 tsp garam masala

2 tbsp chopped coriander (cilantro)
   leaves, to garnish

Put the lentils in a large saucepan with the garlic, turmeric and ginger. Add the stock or water. Stir well, bring to the boil, reduce the heat, cover and simmer for 25–30 minutes until pulpy and the water has been absorbed, stirring occasionally.

After 15 minutes, heat the oil in a pan. Add the onion and fry for about 5 minutes, stirring, until golden and cooked through. Stir in the remaining ingredients except the coriander (cilantro) leaves and fry for 30 seconds. Remove from the heat.

When the lentils are cooked, stir in the onion mixture and serve hot, garnished with the chopped coriander.

SWEET POTATO FRIES

These fries are lower GI than using ordinary potatoes and, being baked in the oven in milk instead of using oil, are low-fat too – a win-win!

Serves 4

2 tbsp milk
1 tsp sweet paprika
2 tsp chopped rosemary leaves (optional)
freshly ground black pepper
4 medium sweet potatoes, scrubbed and cut into thick slices then finger-size strips
rosemary sprig, to garnish

Preheat the oven to 230°C/450°F/Gas 8 and line a baking (cookie) sheet with nonstick baking parchment.

Whisk the milk with the paprika, rosemary, if using, and a good grinding of black pepper in a large, shallow bowl. Add the sweet potato fingers and toss well.

Drain off any excess milk from the sweet potatoes, then spread them out on the prepared baking sheet in a single layer. Bake in the oven for about 20 minutes until golden and tender, turning once or twice. Serve hot, garnished with a sprig of rosemary.

RED CABBAGE CRUNCH

This is yet another dish that sits pretty well on its own for a snack lunch but is also the perfect accompaniment to cold chicken, meat or cheese.

Serves 4

½ red cabbage, finely shredded

1 large carrot cut into matchsticks or coarsely grated

1 small red onion, halved and very thinly sliced

1 handful walnut pieces, roughly chopped if too large

1 handful raisins

1 handful parsley, chopped

4 tbsp light vinaigrette dressing (*see* page 182)

Mix all the salad ingredients together in a bowl. Spoon the dressing over the salad, toss and, if you have time, leave to stand for an hour to allow the flavours to develop. Toss again and garnish with chopped parsley before serving.

SEEDED SPELT SODA BREAD

This quick bread is great to make when time is short and is perfect served warm from the oven. You can just break it into quarters before slicing, so the rest of the bread stays intact. It is best served fresh or toasted the next day.

Makes 1 loaf

450 g/1 lb/3 cups stoneground spelt or wholemeal (whole grain) flour, plus extra for dusting

4 tbsp sunflower seeds

2 tsp bicarbonate of soda (baking soda)

2 tsp cream of tartar

good pinch of salt (optional)

2 tbsp rapeseed (canola) or sunflower oil

300 ml/½ pint/1¼ cups milk

butter, to serve

Preheat the oven to 220°C/425°F/Gas 7 and line a baking (cookie) sheet with baking parchment.

Mix the flour with 3 tablespoons of the sunflower seeds, the bicarbonate of soda (baking soda), cream of tartar and salt, if using. Stir in the oil with a fork, then use your hands to work in enough milk to form a soft but not sticky dough.

Dust your hands with a little more flour and draw the dough together into a ball. Do not handle any more than necessary. Place on the baking sheet and make a deep cross in the top with a sharp knife. Brush lightly with a little more milk and sprinkle with the remaining sunflower seeds. Bake in the oven for about 25 minutes, or until golden and risen and the base sounds hollow with tapped on the base (use oven gloves (mitts) to pick it up). Cool for at least 10 minutes on a wire rack, otherwise it will be difficult to cut, then serve sliced, spread with a scraping of butter, if you like.

TOMATO KETCHUP

Homemade tomato ketchup is full of flavour and packed with lycopene – an antioxidant thought to promote a healthy heart – and no additives. It is best to keep it chunky, but you can rub it through a sieve if you prefer.

Makes 1 small jar

500 g/1 lb 1 oz very ripe, red tomatoes
   (any shape or size), roughly chopped
1 small carrot, chopped
1 shallot, chopped
1 small celery stalk, chopped
pinch of ground cloves

1 bay leaf
good grating of fresh nutmeg
1 tbsp tomato purée (paste)
5 tbsp cider vinegar
a little clear honey (optional)

Put all the ingredients except the honey in a heavy-based saucepan. Bring to the boil, then reduce the heat, cover and simmer gently for 30 minutes. Remove the lid and boil rapidly for a further 10 minutes until pulpy, stirring occasionally.

Discard the bay leaf. Purée the mixture, ideally in a high-speed blender, to break up all the skins or use a stick blender or a food processor. For best health benefits, leave with the bits in, but, for a smoother texture, rub it through a sieve to remove the skins and seeds. Return to the rinsed-out pan and stir in a little honey to taste, if liked. Bring back to the boil and cook for about 5 minutes, stirring until really thickened.

Spoon the ketchup into a sterilised jar. Cover with a circle of baking parchment, then screw on the lid. Leave to cool, then label and store in a cool, dark place for up to 3 months. Once opened, store in the refrigerator and use within two weeks.

HERBY PESTO

This is a delicious chunky pesto to stir through cooked pasta, smear over meat, fish or chicken before grilling (broiling), to flavour dips or dressings or to spread on wholegrain crackers, toasted sourdough or other rustic bread. Thin it with a little hot water before use as a pasta sauce. You can also make it with fresh basil if you prefer.

Makes 1 small jar

4 tbsp olive oil

1 small bunch coriander (cilantro) (about 20 g/¾ oz/¾ cup), leaves picked

1 small bunch flat-leaf parsley (about 20 g/¾ oz/¾ cup), leaves picked

1 large garlic clove, lightly crushed

40 g/1½ oz/¼ cup pine nuts (kernels)

freshly ground black pepper

40g/1½ oz/⅓ cup Parmesan, freshly grated

Reserve 1 tablespoon of the olive oil, then put the remaining ingredients in a bowl, if using a stick blender, or in a food processor. Blend, stopping and scraping down the sides as necessary, until amalgamated into a fragrant, chunky, glistening paste. Pack into a sterilized screw-top jar. Pour the remaining olive oil over the sauce to protect it from the air. Screw on the lid and store in the refrigerator.

LIGHT VINAIGRETTE DRESSING

A great oil-free and sugar-free dressing for all salads, this keeps well in the refrigerator. Less acidic than other vinegars, you'll find white balsamic condiment with the vinegars in your supermarket. You can substitute dark balsamic if you prefer, but it will be darker and sharper.

Makes 1 small bottle

6 tbsp white balsamic condiment

4 tbsp water

1 shallot, very finely chopped

1 tsp Dijon or grainy mustard

¼ tsp dried tarragon or oregano

freshly ground black pepper

Put all the ingredients in a screw-top jar, screw on the lid and shake vigorously until well blended. Store in the refrigerator and use as required.

SIMPLE VEGETABLE STOCK

You can use any well-washed vegetables or vegetable peelings for a stock, but here's a basic recipe to start you off.

Makes about 1 litre/1¾ pints/1 quart

1 leek, thickly sliced

1 large carrot, thickly sliced

2 celery stalks, thickly sliced (outer stalks are fine)

1 onion, roughly chopped

a few mushroom stalks or 1 piece dried mushroom

1 tomato, quartered

¼ small swede (rutabaga), cut in smallish chunks

1 bouquet garni

1.5 litres/2½ pints/1½ quarts water

Put all the ingredients in a large saucepan, cover and bring to the boil, checking frequently so it doesn't boil over. Reduce the heat and simmer gently for 30–40 minutes. Strain, pressing the cooked vegetables well against the side of the strainer to extract the maximum flavour. Leave to cool completely, then store in a covered container in the refrigerator and use as required.

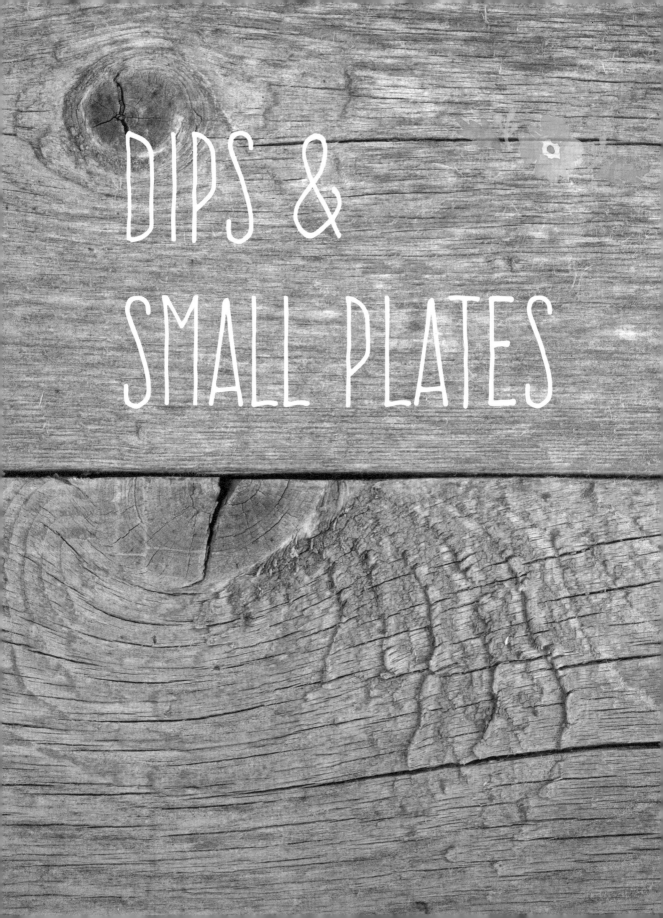

DIPS & SMALL PLATES

BEETROOT HOUMOUS

You can either cook your own beetroot or buy cooked vacuum-packed beetroot, but do make sure it is not pickled. The pastry sticks are an optional extra.

Serves 4

250 g/9 oz cooked beetroot, trimmed and roughly chopped

400 g/14 oz/1 large can chickpeas (garbanzo beans), drained and rinsed

1 garlic clove, peeled and crushed

2 tbsp tahini

juice of ½ lemon

2 tsp ground cumin

2 tbsp chopped thyme

freshly ground black pepper

4 tbsp olive oil

1 tbsp low-fat crème fraîche

1 tbsp white sesame seeds

1 tbsp brown sesame seeds

For the pastry sticks

250 g/9 oz ready-rolled sheet of reduced-fat puff pastry

1 egg, lightly beaten

a little flour, for dusting

To make the pastry sticks, preheat the oven to 200°C/400°F/Gas 6 and line a baking (cookie) sheet with nonstick baking parchment.

Flatten the pastry on the prepared baking sheet, then cut into short, narrow strips, separating them slightly as you do so. Brush with egg, then bake in the oven for about 10 minutes until lightly golden. Transfer to a wire rack to cool.

Meanwhile, put the beetroot, chickpeas, garlic, tahini, lemon juice and ground cumin in a blender or food processor and blitz until blended but still quite chunky. Add half the thyme and some pepper and process again. Gradually add just enough oil to achieve the consistency you prefer.

Spoon into individual ramekins (custard cups) or into one serving dish, swirl in the crème fraîche, then sprinkle with the remaining thyme and the sesame seeds. Serve with the pastry sticks.

TZATZIKI DIP

This refreshing cucumber dip can be served with vegetable sticks or a few puff pastry sticks (*see* page 186) instead of pitta breads, if you prefer.

Serves 4

½ large cucumber

2 garlic cloves, peeled and crushed

350 g/12 oz/1½ cups fat-free plain Greek yogurt

2 tbsp rapeseed (canola) oil

1 tbsp lemon juice, or more to taste

freshly ground black pepper

wholemeal (whole grain) pitta breads, lightly toasted

Grate the cucumber into a sieve (strainer) and press out some of the water. Leave to drain while you prepare the garlic and blend it into the yogurt.

Mix in the oil and lemon juice, then stir in the cucumber until well mixed. Season to taste with pepper and a little more lemon juice, if you like.

Serve with triangles of warm, lightly toasted pitta bread.

BABA GANOUSH

Full of antioxidants that are thought to combat harmful free radicals in the body, aubergines (eggplants) are also high in fibre, low in carbs and so have a low GI, can help lower blood cholesterol and are rich in vitamins and minerals.

Serves 4

500 g/1 lb 1 oz aubergines (eggplants)
½ tsp ground cumin
1 tbsp lemon juice
4 tbsp olive oil
freshly ground black pepper
2 tbsp sesame seeds
sprig flat-leaf parsley leaves
vegetable sticks, to serve

Preheat the oven to 200°C/400°F/Gas 6 and line a baking (cookie) sheet with nonstick baking parchment.

Cut the aubergines (eggplants) in half lengthways. Cut off a thin slice from the rounded base, if necessary, so that it sits flat, then put on the prepared baking sheet and bake for about 30 minutes until soft. Leave until cool enough to handle, then peel and roughly dice the flesh.

Transfer to a blender or food processor, add the cumin, lemon juice and half the oil. Season with pepper. Process until smooth, adding half the remaining oil, if necessary, to reach a soft, smooth consistency.

Spoon into a bowl, sprinkle with the remaining oil and the sesame seeds and serve garnished with the parsley and with plenty of vegetable sticks for dipping.

SOCCA PIZZA WITH FETA

The base for this great snack is made with chickpea (gram) flour. If you prefer a moister top, use small, torn pieces of fresh mozzarella instead of the feta.

Serves 4

For the base

125 g/4 oz/1 cup + 1 tbsp chickpea (gram) flour

2 garlic cloves, peeled and crushed

4 tbsp olive oil

250 ml/8 fl oz/1 cup water

oil spray (optional)

For the topping

1 tbsp sundried tomatoes, chopped

4 ripe tomatoes, chopped

150 g/5 oz thin, tenderstem broccoli (broccolini)

100 g/3½ oz/⅔ cups feta, crumbled

freshly ground black pepper

1 large handful pea shoots

To make the base, stir together the flour, garlic and 2 tbsp of the olive oil, then gradually whisk in the water until you have a smooth, thick batter. Leave to rest at room temperature for about an hour.

Preheat the grill (broiler) to high and put a flameproof frying pan (skillet) under the grill to heat. Use oven gloves to pick up the handle. Preheat the oven to 220°C/425°G/Gas 7 and line a baking (cookie) sheet with nonstick baking parchment.

Spray the pan lightly with oil. Swirl the pan as you gradually pour in enough batter to cover the bottom. Return it to the grill and cook for about 5 minutes until set and golden. Repeat with the remaining batter.

Transfer the bases to the prepared baking sheet. Top with the sundried tomatoes, tomatoes, broccoli and feta and season with pepper. Bake for about 10 minutes until the cheese is lightly golden. Sprinkle with the pea shoots to serve.

MACKEREL PÂTÉ

Mackerel contains plenty of omega-3 fatty acids, which are good for you to eat a couple of times a week. You could also use drained canned sardines in water or use canned or fresh salmon.

Serves 4

100 g/3½ oz cooked mackerel fillets, flaked, discarding skin and any bones
1 small garlic clove, finely chopped
3 tbsp low-fat cream cheese
1½ tbsp horseradish sauce
½ tsp finely grated lemon zest
1 lemon, cut into wedges
freshly ground black pepper
4 slices granary (whole wheat) bread
12 flat-leaf parsley sprigs

Mix together the mackerel, garlic, cream cheese, horseradish and lemon zest. Taste and season with a squeeze of lemon juice, if liked, and plenty of pepper. Cut the bread into circles, using a small biscuit (cookie) cutter (or simply remove the crusts and cut each slice in quarters), spread a spoonful of the pâté over each piece of bread, then top with a parsley leaf and serve with a wedge of lemon.

Alternatively, simply serve the pâté in ramekins (custard cups) with slices of bread on the side.

COURGETTE & CHICKPEA FRITTERS

It is always useful to have cans of chickpeas (garbanzo beans) on hand, but you can also cook your own (*see* notes). This does take a while though, so it's worth cooking a panful then freezing in measured batches for use on other occasions.

Serves 4

4 courgettes (zucchini), grated

400 g/14 oz can chickpeas (garbanzo beans), drained and rinsed

100 g/3½ oz/scant 1 cup chickpea (gram) flour

2 eggs, lightly beaten

3 spring onions (scallions), thinly sliced

1 tsp grated fresh root ginger

1 chili, deseeded and chopped

3 tbsp chopped coriander (cilantro) leaves

freshly ground black pepper

4 tbsp fat-free plain Greek yogurt or low-fat crème fraîche

a little milk (optional)

1 tbsp finely chopped dill

oil spray (optional)

Put the courgettes (zucchini) in a sieve (strainer) and press to remove excess water. Pat dry on kitchen (paper) towel.

Put the chickpeas (garbanzo beans) in a food processor with the courgettes, flour, eggs, spring onions (scallions), ginger, chili and half the coriander (cilantro). Season with pepper. Pulse to a thick batter, adding a little milk, if necessary. If you prefer a chunkier fritter, crush the ingredients together in a bowl with a potato masher.

Heat a large frying pan and spray with a little oil, if you like. Add tablespoonfuls of the mixture, well apart, and fry for about 3 minutes until browned on the underside. Flip them over and cook the other side. Repeat until you have used all the mixture, keeping the cooked fritters warm in a low oven.

Stack the fritters and put a spoonful of yogurt on top. Sprinkle with the dill and the remaining coriander and serve hot.

Notes

To cook dried chicpeas, soak the chickpeas overnight, then drain, put in a saucepan and fill with water to come 5 cm/2 inches above the chickpeas. Add a bay leaf and a peeled and crushed garlic clove, bring to the boil and boil for 10 minutes, then reduce the heat and simmer for about 2 hours or until tender. Drain and use as required.

PAPRIKA DEVILLED EGGS

These retro treats take a little while to prepare but make an eye-catching starter or nibbles to serve with drinks.

Serves 4

12 eggs
4 tbsp low-fat mayonnaise
1 tsp Dijon mustard
½ tsp paprika
a few drops Tabasco sauce
1½ tsp olive oil
freshly ground black pepper
3 tbsp freshly boiled water
1 tbsp finely snipped chives
a few mixed olives, sliced

Put the eggs in a large saucepan, cover with cold water, bring to the boil, then simmer for 10 minutes. Drain and refresh under cold water until cool enough to handle.

Peel the eggs, halve lengthways and put the yolks into a bowl. Arrange the whites on a plate; if preferred, slice off a sliver from the base of each to make them stand upright. Gently crush the egg yolks, then blend in the mayonnaise, mustard, half the paprika, the tabasco and olive oil and season to taste with pepper. Use a stick blender for a really smooth mix. Add enough water to make a piping consistency.

Pipe the mixture into the egg whites, or simply pile in using two teaspoons, then top with the chives and olives and a sprinkling of the remaining paprika.

DUKKHA

There are any number of variations you can make with this Egyptian mixture of nuts, seeds and spices. Try sprinkling on the flatbreads, drizzling with a little oil and baking until crisp.

Serves 4

35 g/1¼ oz/¼ cup hazelnuts

4 tbsp sesame seeds

2 tbsp coriander seeds

1 tbsp cumin seeds

1 tbsp freshly ground black pepper

a little coarsely ground sea salt (optional)

1 tsp ground cinnamon

1 tsp chopped thyme leaves (optional)

wholegrain pittas or other flatbreads, to serve

olive oil, to serve

Toast the hazelnuts in a small, dry saucepan until toasted and aromatic, shaking the pan occasionally. Tip them into a spice grinder or mortar and crush, not too finely. Tip into a bowl.

Toast the sesame, coriander and cumin seeds in the same way, then add them to the grinder or mortar. Add the pepper, a little salt, if you like, the cinnamon and thyme, if using, then grind or crush finely. Mix them with the hazelnuts.

Serve with a bowl of good olive oil and some pittas or other flatbreads to dip into the oil, and then into the dukkha.

DESSERTS & SWEET TREATS

FROZEN MANGO YOGURT

Serving this refreshing dessert as soon as it is made will give a creamy result, while freezing the dessert will give a firmer finish. Remember that mango is very sweet, so factor that into what you eat that day.

Serves 4

1 ripe mango, peeled, pitted and roughly chopped

1 small banana, peeled

250 g/8 oz/1 cup fat-free plain Greek yogurt

finely grated zest and juice of ½ lime, or to taste

1 small handful pistachios, roughly chopped

Put the prepared mango and the banana in the freezer overnight.

Transfer the fruit to the bowl of a food processor, add the yogurt, lime zest and juice and process until smooth. Spoon into individual dishes and sprinkle with the pistachios to serve.

If you don't want to serve it all, spoon the remaining mixture into a freezerproof container and place in the freezer.

BAKED PEACHES
with Star Anise

Substitute nectarines if you prefer and sprinkle with ground cinnamon. You can buy freeze-dried raspberries in the baking aisle of major supermarkets.

Serves 4

8 tbsp fruity white wine or cider (hard, not apple juice)

1 cinnamon stick

6 star anise

4 ripe peaches, halved and pitted

2 tbsp freeze-dried raspberries or strawberries, crushed (optional)

1 handful flaked (slivered) almonds

Preheat the oven to 190°C/375°F/Gas 5 and line a baking pan with baking parchment.

Put the wine or cider (hard cider) and spices in a saucepan and bring to the boil. Simmer for
10 minutes or so until syrupy.

Sit the peaches, skin-side down, in the prepared baking pan and spoon the syrup and spices over the top. Bake for about 15 minutes until the peaches are soft and golden, watching carefully to make sure they don't burn. Serve sprinkled with the crushed raspberries or strawberries, if using, and the almonds.

STRAWBERRY CHEESECAKE POTS

This is similar to Eton Mess but with nuts and oats instead of the sugary meringue.
You could use 4 crushed Marie biscuits (vanilla wafers) and 2 tablespoons
ground almonds instead.

Serves 4

50 g/2 oz/½ cup whole raw almonds or other nuts

2 tbsp rolled oats

pinch ground cinnamon

300 g/10½ oz strawberries, hulled

250 g/8 oz/1 cup fat-free plain Greek yogurt

150 g/5 oz/⅔ cup low-fat cream cheese

few drops vanilla extract

a few mint leaves

Put the nuts in a dry pan and toss over a medium to high heat for a few minutes until
browned and aromatic, shaking the pan occasionally. Tip them out of the pan and
leave to cool, then chop roughly. Mix with the oats and cinnamon.

Slice 4 or 5 strawberries thinly and put them in the bottom of four serving glasses.
Halve the remaining strawberries.

Whisk together the yogurt, cream cheese and vanilla, then spoon the mixture over the
strawberries. Top with the nut mixture, then pile the remaining strawberries on top and
garnish with mint leaves to serve.

APPLE, BLUEBERRY & RASPBERRY CRISP

A new take on a classic; try this with different fruits. You could toast whole nuts, then chop them to add crunch. Leftovers are great cold for breakfast with some fat-free plain Greek yogurt.

Serves 4

2 large cooking apples, such as Bramleys (or Rome Beauty), peeled, cored and sliced
125 g/4 oz/1 cup blueberries
150 g/5 oz/1½ cups raspberries
squeeze of lemon juice
250 g/9 oz/2½ cups low-sugar granola
low-fat crème fraîche, to serve

Preheat the oven to 160°C/325°F/Gas 3.

Rinse the fruit in water, then drain, leaving the fruit with just the water on the skins. Tip into a baking dish and sprinkle with the lemon juice.

Spoon the granola over the fruit and bake for 30–40 minutes until the fruit is soft and the topping golden. Serve with a spoonful of crème fraîche, if liked.

CARROT & LEMON MUFFINS

Make sure you don't overwork the mixture when you are making muffins. Stop stirring as soon as the dry ingredients are blended into the wet. Muffins are best cooked and eaten on the same day.

Makes 12 muffins

2 ripe bananas, mashed

250 g/9 oz/2 cups wholemeal (whole grain) flour

½ tsp bicarbonate of soda (baking soda)

½ tsp ground cinnamon

100 g/3½ oz/1 cup rolled oats, plus extra for sprinkling

2 carrots, grated

75 g/3 oz/½ cup sultanas (golden raisins)

2 eggs

50 ml/2 fl oz/¼ cup sunflower oil

finely grated zest and juice of 1 lemon

250 ml/8 fl oz/1 cup oat or skimmed milk

low-fat crème fraiche or fat-free plain Greek yogurt, to serve

Preheat the oven to 190°C/375°F/Gas 5 and line a 12-hole muffin pan with paper cases.

Mix together the bananas, flour, bicarbonate of soda (baking soda), cinnamon, oats, carrots and sultanas (golden raisins). In a separate bowl, whisk the eggs, oil, lemon zest, juice and milk. Pour into the dry ingredients and mix gently until just blended, adding a little extra milk if needed to make a light, spoonable mixture – don't overwork or the muffins will be hard.

Spoon into the prepared cases and sprinkle with a few oats. Bake for about 20 minutes until risen, golden and springy when pressed. Serve warm or cold on their own or with a spoonful of crème fraiche or yogurt.

CHOCOLATE ORANGE BEETROOT BROWNIES

Beetroot is a delicious vegetable that works just as well in cakes as the more familiar carrot. To save cooking, you could use vacuum-packed cooked beetroot.

Makes about 15 brownies

3 small raw beetroot
200 g/7 oz 70 per cent dark (bittersweet) chocolate, broken into pieces
100 ml/3½ fl oz/scant ⅓ cup sunflower oil
100 g/3½ oz/½ cup soft, light brown sugar
3 eggs

160 g/5½ oz/heaped 1 cup wholemeal (whole grain) flour
1 tsp baking powder
grated zest and juice of 1 orange
few freeze-dried raspberries, crushed, to decorate

Put the beetroot in a saucepan, cover with water and bring to the boil. Cover and simmer for about 25 minutes until tender to the point of a knife, then drain, trim and blend to a purée. Preheat the oven to 180°C/350°F/Gas 4 and line a 15 x 23-cm/6 x 9-in rectangular baking pan with baking parchment. Melt the chocolate in a heatproof bowl set over a pan of gently simmering water. Remove from the heat and add the oil.

Beat the sugar and eggs in a separate bowl until smooth. Stir in the puréed beetroot, the chocolate and oil mixture, the flour, baking powder and orange zest. Gradually add enough of the orange juice to make a smooth, thick batter. Spoon the batter into the prepared pan and bake for about 30 minutes until firm to the touch. Check after 25 minutes if you like a brownie with a very soft middle. Leave to cool in the pan for 10 minutes, then transfer to a wire rack to cool. Sprinkle with the crushed raspberries and cut into squares to serve.

PEANUT BUTTER & CHOCOLATE COOKIES

You can make these cookies with or without the chocolate. Either way, they are deliciously crumbly. They freeze well too.

Makes about 12 cookies

30 g/1 oz/¼ cup walnuts

40 g/1½ oz dark (semisweet dark) chocolate, roughly chopped

250 g/9 oz/1 cup crunchy peanut butter (with no added ingredients)

125 g/4 oz/½ cup soft, dark brown sugar

150 g/5 oz/1½ cups rolled oats

½ tsp bicarbonate of soda (baking soda)

2 eggs, lightly beaten

Preheat the oven to 180°C/350°F/Gas 4 and line a baking (cookie) sheet with baking parchment.

Put the walnuts in a pan over a medium to high heat and toast until browned and aromatic, shaking the pan occasionally. Tip out onto a board, leave to cool slightly, then chop. Melt the chocolate in a heatproof bowl set over a pan of gently simmering water.

Mix together all the ingredients except the walnuts. Shape spoonfuls of the mixture on the prepared baking sheet, then gently flatten using a fork and sprinkle with the walnuts. Bake for 12–15 minutes until browned on top. Leave to cool on the baking sheet for a few minutes before transferring to a wire rack to finish cooling.

DATE & PISTACHIO BITES

So quick to put together, these sweet little bites make a lovely end to a meal, or a treat to keep up your energy if you have a long gap between meals. They are high in natural sugar, so one or two a day is enough.

Makes about 12 bites

75g/3 oz/½ cup pitted dates

60 g/2¼ oz/½ cup raisins

2 carrots, finely grated

60 g/2¼ oz/½ cup rolled oats

1 tsp ground cinnamon

1 pinch freshly grated nutmeg

50 g/2 oz/scant ½ cup unsalted pistachios, chopped

2–3 tbsp skimmed, almond or oat milk

Put the dates, raisins, carrots, oats, cinnamon, nutmeg and half the pistachios in a food processor and blend until chopped and well mixed. Process again, gradually adding enough milk until the mixture starts to stick together.

With wet hands, to prevent the mixture sticking to you, roll into about 12 small balls. Put the remaining pistachios in a wide, shallow dish and roll the balls in the nuts, pressing them into the mixture. Store in the fridge.

INDEX

Entries with upper-case initials indicate recipes.

If you enjoyed this book please sign up for updates,
information and offers on further titles in this series at
www.flametreepublishing.com